The Holt Reader
Adapted Version

Teacher's Guide and Answer Key

Introductory Through Second Course

Isabel L. Beck, Ph.D., Program Consultant

HOLT, RINEHART AND WINSTON

ISBN 978-0-03-099646-7
ISBN 0-03-099646-5

3 4 5 179 11 10 09 08

Contents

Appendix

To the Teacher

Welcome to the Program

The Holt Reader, Adapted Version is a consumable book designed to accompany *Elements of Literature*, where the original versions of these selections appear. Most of the selections have been adapted, or retold, to make the text more accessible to struggling readers. That is, the selections' vocabulary and sentence structure have been simplified. In the process of adapting these selections, great care has been taken to maintain the selections' flavor and tone.

Instruction is also targeted to readers gaining proficiency. In *The Holt Reader, Adapted Version*, extra support before, throughout, and after the selection helps the struggling reader gain more meaning and enjoyment from the text.

Students who need extra support while working in the main anthology will find that using *The Holt Reader, Adapted Version* helps them move with the rest of the class in reading aloud, discussions, writing assignments, and projects. *The Holt Reader, Adapted Version* can also be used for independent practice. Clear directions, uncomplicated format, and consistent instruction make this book an ideal tool for effective homework or for students who need additional help.

A special aspect of *The Holt Reader, Adapted Version* is the inclusion of the Questioning the Author (QtA) concept developed by Dr. Isabel L. Beck and Dr. Margaret G. McKeown. In this book, the QtA queries have been labeled Read and Discuss. For more information on how Questioning the Author is used here, see the essay by Dr. Beck and Dr. McKeown on page vii.

The Minimum Course of Study

Elements of Literature is designed to help you meet your state and local curricula as well as to provide you with a wide range of materials from which to choose. One concern many teachers have is making sure that, while choosing from that wide range of materials, they do not inadvertently overlook any necessary skills or state standards.

To help teachers meet this challenge, Holt, Rinehart and Winston developed a Minimum Course of Study. First, we examined the reading, vocabulary, and literary standards from states throughout the country and identified the scope and sequence of skills that must be covered in order to meet those standards. Then, with that scope and sequence in hand, we identified the core selections that could be used to cover all those standards. We call that core the Minimum Course of Study (MCOS) because it represents the most direct path through the student materials, a path that will ensure coverage of state standards and essential skills related to reading, vocabulary, and literature. The MCOS includes all genres of literature—short stories, essays, poems, drama—as well as informational texts.

Because *The Holt Reader, Adapted Version* is designed for struggling readers and English learners, the table of contents reflects the Minimum Course of Study. If your students read all of the selections in *The Holt Reader, Adapted Version*, and master the skills related to those selections, they will have mastered state reading, vocabulary, and literary standards.

Guiding Principles of the Program

The development of *The Holt Reader, Adapted Version* was guided by several principles:

- Students need explicit and systematic instruction to unlock the meaning of literary and informational text and to develop reading skills.

- Students need to interact with the text in order to access the meaning and power of the printed word and develop positive attitudes toward reading.

- Students need to read a wide range of materials to become comfortable with the many text structures they will encounter in their daily lives.

- To master language arts skills, students need to understand the expectations for each skill and see how the skill applies to what they are reading.

- Students need scaffolded instruction, starting with strong guided support and leading toward independence.

Questioning the Author and *The Holt Reader, Adapted Version*

By Dr. Isabel L. Beck and Dr. Margaret G. McKeown

WHAT IS QUESTIONING THE AUTHOR?

Questioning the Author (QtA) is the name we have given to our approach to comprehension. We developed QtA as a response to our earlier research, research which had demonstrated that too often students had little understanding of what they had read. Among the reasons for students' lack of understanding was that many of them did not *engage* with what they were reading.

Toward supporting students to become engaged with text, QtA incorporated the following key features:

- First, QtA mimics building meaning *during* initial reading, which is essential for successful comprehension, by stopping at points in the text and discussing the important ideas.
- Second, at these stopping points QtA deals with the text under consideration through general queries such as "What is going on with (character) now?" "What picture is the author painting for us?" "What do you think the author means by …?" Such questions signal students that they are responsible for thinking about the text and constructing meaning.
- Third, discussion is focused on the goal of understanding the text. Discussions that survey students' ideas about a text or have students argue their opinions serve a different purpose than that of QtA. The purpose of a QtA discussion is to ensure that students are indeed comprehending what they read by having them look at text through a tighter lens. The teacher is actively involved, right there with the class the whole time, as a facilitator, a guide, an initiator, and a responder. Students' responses to the queries are the building blocks of meaning, meaning that is further developed through teachers' responses to students and students' subsequent elaboration and connections. Thus, the development of meaning in QtA focuses on readers' interactions with text as it is being read, situates reader-text interactions in whole-class discussion, and encourages explanatory, evidence-based responses to questions about text.

HOW IS QtA REFLECTED IN THE INSTRUCTION IN *THE HOLT READER, ADAPTED VERSION*?

In *The Holt Reader*, *Adapted Version* questions under the label Read and Discuss appear in the sidebars. The **type**, **style**, and **sequence** of the Read and Discuss questions were derived from QtA queries.

The **type** of these questions is open in that the questions are designed to prompt students to consider text *ideas* rather than merely retrieve text *words*. These questions often require students to connect text ideas. For example, in "Amigo Brothers," *The Holt Reader*, *Adapted Version*, page 4, we use the question, "How does the boys' decision to train separately add to what we know about Felix and Antonio?" To answer this question, students need not only to have understood that the friends want the fight to be fair, but also to have connected that motivation to the kind of positive and decent young men that Felix and Antonio are. Or consider the question, "What can we learn from the conversation between the boys and their trainers?" This question requires students to infer that each trainer is encouraging his boxer to use his strengths against the other's weakness. In contrast, a question such as, "What are the trainers telling their boxers?" would merely encourage a recitation of what the trainers told them. Felix's trainer tells him "to get in close," and Antonio's trainer tells him, "Felix always goes for the body." Such a recitation does not lead students to make connections and understand meaning.

The **style** of the QtA questions, or queries, is not formal. QtA questions are designed to prompt a conversation, not to formally elicit a right or wrong answer. That style was adopted for the Read and Discuss questions in *The Holt Reader*, *Adapted Version*.

In addition, the **sequence** for QtA questions follows the chain of events and ideas in a text, along with the interrelationships between the events and ideas. This sequencing supports students in building coherent understanding. The Read and Discuss questions in *The Holt Reader*, *Adapted Version* are sequenced accordingly.

HOW DO I USE THE READ AND DISCUSS QUESTIONS IN THE CLASSROOM?

Using the Student Work Text. There are several ways that the Read and Discuss questions can be used in the classroom. The preferred approach is that the teacher and students work through a text together. That is, you invite different students to read a portion of text aloud and then stop the reading at the point of a sidebar Read and Discuss question and ask the question. The question then triggers discussion in which students are urged to grapple with ideas in the service of constructing meaning. This process of alternating reading and discussion illustrates to students that building meaning from text is an iterative process in which ideas are considered as they are offered.

A second approach delays the discussion until after the students have read the selection. During-reading discussion has been shown to be particularly beneficial to students' comprehension, but after-reading discussion also has benefits. So, if you prefer that students work through the Read and Discuss questions on their own, the teacher-student discussion can occur when the written responses are completed. With this approach, it is appropriate to allow students to alter their responses based on the discussion.

Using This *Teacher's Guide and Answer Key*. This teacher's guide also includes two features that will help you use the Read and Discuss questions effectively in your classroom. The first feature identifies a major comprehension goal for a text. These goals, which are labeled Major Understanding for Read and Discuss Queries, are located at the beginning of the answers for each selection. The second feature combines an explanation of the way in which each question contributes to building meaning from the story with the question and its possible answer. Let's take a look at how these two features work.

We'll start with the Major Understanding provided for "Amigo Brothers" in this teacher's guide:

"Amigo Brothers" explores the complicated world of Antonio and Felix, who are best friends and boxing competitors. Antonio and Felix demonstrate that honor in boxing and honor in friendship can be achieved simultaneously.

That statement captures the essence of the higher-level understanding of the selection. It is not a summary, but an encapsulation of where the major ideas may lead a reader. For the teacher, the Major Understanding is a kind of framework around which the discussion should develop. We have suggested thinking of the Major Understanding as the way we might want a student to describe what he had read in school that day to his family at the dinner table.

The second feature in this guide provides a statement that tells why each Read and Discuss question is being asked (its purpose), followed by the question, and finally a possible response. For example, let's consider the three parts provided in the *Teacher's Guide* for another question from "Amigo Brothers":

[Purpose] *To understand that each boy finds a way to imagine he is the winner of the match*: [Question] **What are the boys up to now?** (Possible response: Each one has come up with a way to focus on winning the match—to visualize being the champion while imagining the other as the loser.)

Those three components of a Read and Discuss question—purpose, question, and possible response—provide tools you can use to support your students as they work out the answer to a question. For instance, if you ask the question as presented and get inadequate answers, you can use your knowledge of the purpose of the question to guide the rewording of the question. Moreover, the possible response suggests the information, or answer, that you need to elicit in order to help your students build and connect key ideas. With that goal in mind, you will be able to develop questions and follow-ups to scaffold students' understanding.

Key Strategies for Helping Readers Gain Proficiency

Even if you are not a trained reading teacher, there are many excellent reading strategies you can use to help struggling readers in your classroom. The instruction in *The Holt Reader, Adapted Version* program is based on two of the best ways to improve students' reading comprehension—modeling thinking aloud and building student fluency.

Think-Alouds

In a Think-Aloud, students pause in their reading from time to time to think aloud about what connections they are making to the text, what images they see, what questions they have, and how they might answer them. This strategy allows you to understand where a student is having difficulty, and it helps the student analyze his or her own reading process. The side-column notes in *The Holt Reader, Adapted Version* help students think through, react, and respond to the text in several different ways as they proceed through the selection, rather than only at the end of the text. You may want to encourage students to read these notes aloud.

You can build on the instruction in *The Holt Reader, Adapted Version* by practicing Think-Alouds in the classroom. To model a Think-Aloud, tell students that you will be reading aloud and stopping from time to time to think about what you have just read. As you read to the class, stop often to talk about how you are analyzing the text. Some of the things you might be doing are visualizing, asking questions, comparing, decoding unfamiliar words, or predicting what comes next. When you switch from reading to thinking aloud, be sure to give students a cue, either verbal or visual, that you're switching. When you have modeled this process several times, have students try it themselves with a partner. Encourage students to think aloud often, and continue to model the process for them regularly.

Fluency

Like thinking aloud, building fluency requires practice. Fluency is the ability to read at a smooth pace and with expression. Struggling readers often pause between words. They skip over punctuation, and they read very, very slowly. To achieve fluency, struggling readers must practice reading at every opportunity—reading, re-reading, reading aloud, reading along. Here are some ways to help students build fluency:

- To improve reading speed, work with students to master sight words and high-frequency words. Sight words are words readers need to know "on sight" because the words don't follow normal decoding rules. High-frequency words are common to a variety of texts. For your convenience, six lists of high-frequency words—starting with the simplest and advancing to the more difficult—are provided in the Appendix of this *Teacher's Guide and Answer Key*. Have students practice recognizing and sounding out these words.

- Let students hear the texts they are reading. Read aloud to the class, modeling appropriate expression, phrasing, and pacing. Invite students to read aloud individually or in choral readings.
- Teach students how to read aloud. Point out how internal punctuation affects the phrasing of a sentence and how end punctuation affects inflection. You can perform simple experiments with the class by adding, changing, or deleting punctuation from the same sentence.
- Have students re-read a text aloud several times. Once students have read and understood a passage, they can turn their attention to working on phrasing and pacing in subsequent readings.
- Don't immediately supply the correct word. When a student pauses over a word, give him or her time to figure it out. If the student continues to struggle, offer some ways of figuring out the word—looking for word parts, sounding it out, guessing what word would make sense in the context.

For more information on fluency, including appropriate reading passages, see *Differentiating Instruction*, another ancillary for *Elements of Literature*.

Research Bibliography

Alliance for Excellent Education. 2004. *Reading Next: A Vision for Action and Research in Middle and High School Literacy.*

Alliance for Excellent Education. 2007. *Double the Work: Challenges and Solutions to Acquiring Language and Academic Literacy for Adolescent English Language Learners.*

Allington, Richard. *What Really Matters for Struggling Readers: Designing Research-Based Programs.* New York, NY: Addison-Wesley, 2001.

Alvermann, D. E., 2005. "Literacy on the Edge: How Close Are We to Closing the Literacy Achievement Gap?" *Voices from the Middle* 13 (1): pp. 8–14.

Appleman. D. (2000). *Critical Encounters in High School English: Teaching Literary Theory to Adolescents.* New York: Teachers College Press.

August, D., & Shanahan, T., eds. (2006). *Developing Literacy in Second-Language Learners: Report of the National Literacy Panel on Language-Minority Children and Youth.* Mahwah, NJ: Lawrence Erlbaum.

Beck, I. L., McKeown, M. G. (2006) *Building Comprehension During Reading with Questioning the Author: A Fresh and Expanded View of a Powerful Approach.* Scholastic.

Beck, I. L., McKeown, M. G., and Kucan, L. (2002). *Bringing Words to Life: Robust Vocabulary Instruction.* New York: Guilford.

Beck, I. L., McKeown, M. G., Sandora, C., Kucan, L., & Worthy, J. (1996). "Questioning the Author: A Yearlong Classroom Implementation to Engage Students with Text." *Elementary School Journal*, Volume 96, Number 4. pp. 385–414.

Beers, K., Probst, R.E., & Rief, L., eds. (2007). *Adolescent Literacy: Turning Promise into Practice.* Portsmouth, NH: Heinemann.

Beers, Kylene. (2002). *When Kids Can't Read/What Teachers Can Do: A Guide for Teachers Grades 6-12.* Portsmouth, NH: Heinemann.

Blachowicz, C. L. Z., & Fisher, P. (2000). "Vocabulary Instruction." In M. L. Kamil, P. B. Mosenthal, P.D. Pearson, & R. Barr (Eds.). *Handbook of Reading Research* (Vol. 3, pp. 503–524). White Plains, NY: Longman.

Blevins, W. (2001). *Teaching Phonics and Word Study in the Intermediate Grades.* New York: Scholastic.

Block, Cathy and Michael Pressley. *Comprehension Instruction: Research-Based Best Practices*. New York, NY: Guilford Press, 2000.

Fu, D. (2003). *An Island of English: Teaching ESL in Chinatown*. Portsmouth, NH: Heinemann.

Kajder, S. (2003). The Tech-Savvy English Classroom. York: ME. Stenhouse.

Ogle, Donna and Camille Blachowicz. (2002). "Beyond Literature Circles: Helping Students Comprehend Informational Texts." *Comprehension Instruction: Research-Based Best Practices*. Eds. C. Block and M. Pressley. New York, NY: Guilford Press. pp. 259–272.

Pressley, Michael. (2002). "Comprehension Strategies Instruction: A Turn-of-the Century Status Report." *Comprehension Instruction: Research-Based Best Practices*. Eds. C. Block and M. Pressley. New York, NY: Guilford Press. pp. 11–27.

Tatum, A. W. (2005). *Teaching Reading to Black Adolescent Males: Closing the Achievement Gap*. Portland, ME: Stenhouse.

A Walk Through *The Holt Reader, Adapted Version* Student Edition

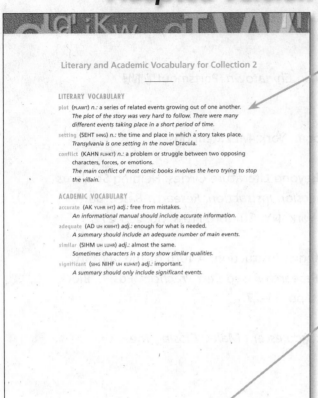

Before Reading the Collection

Literary and Academic Vocabulary

Literary and academic vocabulary refers to the language of books, tests, and formal writing. Each collection begins with the literary and academic terms that students need to master the skills for that collection. The terms for this feature come from the Skills in Action Wrap-Up, Literary Focus, or Reading Model pages in the *Elements of Literature* student edition. The more difficult definitions have been simplified.

Before Reading the Selection

Preparing to Read

Previewing texts builds success. This page prepares students to read the selection. The feature previews the skills and vocabulary they will need to get the most from the reading. Information from the student edition Preparing to Read pages has been condensed to its essentials for this feature. Some short selections share a single Preparing to Read page.

Literary Focus

In literary selections, this feature introduces the literary focus for the selection. The focus echoes what appears in the student edition of *Elements of Literature*. Examples and graphic elements help clarify the literary focus.

Reading Focus

Also in literary selections, this feature highlights a reading skill for students to apply to the selection. The feature points out to students why this skill is important and how it can help them become better readers.

Informational Text Focus

For informational selections, this feature discusses the format and characteristics of nonfiction texts such as newspaper articles, Web sites, employment regulations, and application forms.

Preparing to Read

Rikki-tikki-tavi
Based on the story by Rudyard Kipling

LITERARY FOCUS: CONFLICT

Conflict is the problem or struggle that makes a story interesting. Often, we can explain the main conflict in one phrase, like "hero versus villain." Conflict is worked out in the related events, or **plot**, of a story. The diagram below shows a few of the types of conflicts a story's hero might face.

Hero →
- Villain
- Nature
- Self

READING FOCUS: SUMMARIZE

To **summarize** is to retell a story that someone else has written in your own words. Retell the **main ideas**, or most important events, in your summary. When you summarize a story, one of the first things you need to identify is the main conflict.

VOCABULARY

Work with a partner to practice using these words in complete sentences.

slither (SLITH ER) *v.:* slide from side to side.

scornfully (SKAWRN FUL LEE) *adv.:* with contempt.

coiled (KOY OYLD) *adj.:* gathered in loops or circles.

INTO THE STORY

The following story is set in India during a time when the British government ruled that country. The hero of the story, Rikki-tikki-tavi, is a mongoose. A mongoose is an animal that looks like a cross between a squirrel and a weasel. The story is about a conflict between the mongoose and the deadly snakes that share his yard.

SKILLS FOCUS

Literary Skills
Understand conflict.

Reading Skills
Summarize a text.

RIKKI-TIKKI-TAVI

Based on the story by Rudyard Kipling

© Mira/Alamy

This is the story of a great war. Rikki-tikki-tavi fought this war in an English family's home in India. He had some help, but he did the real fighting.

Rikki-tikki was a mongoose. His name came from the sound he made going into battle: *Rikk-tikk-tikki-tikki-tchk!* **A**

When Rikki was small, a flood swept him away from his home and family. A little boy named Teddy found him half-dead and brought him home. Teddy and his mother warmed the mongoose till he woke up.

10   Although the mother had a soft spot for animals, she wasn't sure she wanted a wild animal in her house. But Teddy's father convinced her that a mongoose was the perfect house pet. After all, deadly snakes lived right in their garden, and mongooses were snake killers. **B**

Rikki-tikki soon felt better, and he spent the rest of the day and the next morning exploring Teddy's house. **C** In the yard he heard the sad voices of two tailorbirds, Darzee and his wife. The birds were crying because a cobra named Nag had eaten one of their babies. **D** Just then, Nag himself appeared. He was a huge

20   black cobra, five feet long.

A READ AND DISCUSS

Comprehension
What has the author told you about Rikki-tikki so far?

B HERE'S HOW

Reading Focus
I will begin by **summarizing** the **main ideas** in lines 1–14. I meet the main character (Rikki-tikki-tavi) and find out how he came to live with Teddy's family.

C HERE'S HOW

Language Coach
I know that the word *exploring* is formed by adding the suffix *–ing* to the **root word** *explore*.

D HERE'S HOW

Literary Focus
I read in lines 16–19 that two birds, Darzee and his wife, are upset. They are upset because a snake named Nag ate one of their babies. I think Nag will continue to cause **conflicts**, or problems, in this story. These conflicts will be important to the **plot**.

Selection Vocabulary
This feature preteaches selection vocabulary. (For informational selections, it appears on the previous page.) Each entry gives the pronunciation and definition of the word.

Into the Story
This feature provides introductory information about the selection related to the author, setting, historical events, or other topics that struggling readers need to make sense of the selection. The feature may appear on the first page of the selection instead of on the Preparing to Read page.

While Reading the Selection

Side-Column Notes
Each selection is accompanied by notes in the side column that guide students' interaction with the selection. Each note has a letter that refers to the place in the text where students should pause for instructional support.

Types of Notes
Several different types of notes throughout the selection provide practice for the skills introduced on the Preparing to Read pages. The types of side-column notes are

- **Read and Discuss** These notes ask readers to pause at certain points so that, through class discussion, teachers can ensure that students understand basic concepts in the text. (See "A Special Message from Isabel Beck, Ph.D." for more information on these notes.)

- **Here's How** This feature shows students how to apply a particular skill to what they are reading. It models how another person might think through the text. Each Here's How addresses the selection's Reading Focus, Literary Focus, Language Coach, or Vocabulary.

- **Your Turn** In these notes, students have a chance to apply vocabulary skills and practice the same reading, literary, and language skills introduced and modeled earlier.

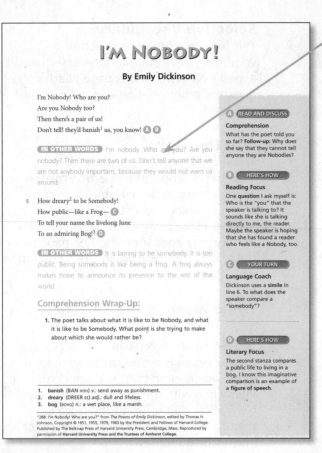

I'M NOBODY!

By Emily Dickinson

I'm Nobody! Who are you?
Are you Nobody too?
Then there's a pair of us!
Don't tell! they'd banish[1] us, you know! **A B**

IN OTHER WORDS I'm nobody. Who are you? Are you nobody? Then there are two of us. Don't tell anyone that we are not anybody important, because they would not want us around.

5 How dreary[2] to be Somebody!
How public—like a Frog— **C**
To tell your name the livelong June
To an admiring Bog![3] **D**

IN OTHER WORDS It is boring to be somebody. It is too public. Being somebody is like being a frog. A frog always makes noise to announce its presence to the rest of the world.

Comprehension Wrap-Up:

1. The poet talks about what it is like to be Nobody, and what it is like to be Somebody. What point is she trying to make about which she would rather be?

---

1. **banish** (BAN IHSH) v.: send away as punishment.
2. **dreary** (DREER EE) adj.: dull and lifeless.
3. **bog** (BOHG) n.: a wet place, like a marsh.

"288: I'm Nobody! Who are you?" from *The Poems of Emily Dickinson*, edited by Thomas H. Johnson. Copyright © 1951, 1955, 1979, 1983 by the President and Fellows of Harvard College. Published by The Belknap Press of Harvard University Press, Cambridge, Mass. Reproduced by permission of **Harvard University Press and the Trustees of Amherst College.**

A READ AND DISCUSS

Comprehension
What has the poet told you so far? **Follow-up:** Why does she say that they cannot tell anyone they are Nobodies?

B HERE'S HOW

Reading Focus
One **question** I ask myself is: Who is the "you" that the speaker is talking to? It sounds like she is talking directly to me, the reader. Maybe the speaker is hoping that she has found a reader who feels like a Nobody, too.

C YOUR TURN

Language Coach
Dickinson uses a **simile** in line 6. To what does the speaker compare a "somebody"?

D HERE'S HOW

Literary Focus
The second stanza compares a public life to living in a bog. I know this imaginative comparison is an example of a **figure of speech.**

In-Text Help

Some selections in *The Holt Reader, Adapted Version* have not been rewritten, for one of three reasons: to comply with the author's wishes, to maintain the graphic nature of the selection, or to retain the original text of plays and poems. So that students receive help with these selections, summaries titled In Other Words are provided.

A READ AND DISCUSS

Comprehension
What is going on between Mr. Frank and Miep?

B HERE'S HOW

Literary Focus
I think that Hitler's coming to power and Anne's family being Jewish will be important elements of the play's major **conflict.** I will keep this in mind as I continue reading.

70 house we lived in . . . the school . . . that street organ playing out there . . . I'm not the person you used to know, Miep. I'm a bitter[12] old man. (*Breaking off*) Forgive me. I shouldn't speak to you like this . . . after all that you did for us . . . the suffering. . . .
Miep. No. No. It wasn't suffering. You can't say we suffered. (*As she speaks, she straightens a chair which is overturned.*)
Mr. Frank. I know what you went through, you and Mr. Kraler. I'll remember it as long as I live. (*He gives one last look around.*) Come, Miep. (*He starts for the steps, then remembers his rucksack, going back to get it.*) **A**
Miep (*hurrying up to a cupboard*). Mr. Frank, did you see? There
80 are some of your papers here. (*She brings a bundle of papers to him.*) We found them in a heap of rubbish on the floor after . . . after you left.
Mr. Frank. Burn them. (*He opens his rucksack to put the glove in it.*)
Miep. But, Mr. Frank, there are letters, notes . . .
Mr. Frank. Burn them. All of them.
Miep. Burn *this*? (*She hands him a paperbound notebook.*)

IN OTHER WORDS Mr. Frank tells Miep that he is leaving Amsterdam. He thanks her for what she and Mr. Kraler did for them while they were in hiding. Miep brings him a pile of his papers, and he says to burn them. He does not want to remember the past.

Mr. Frank (*quietly*). Anne's diary. (*He opens the diary and begins to read.*) "Monday, the sixth of July, nineteen forty-two."
90 (*To* MIEP) Nineteen forty-two. Is it possible, Miep? . . . Only three years ago. (*As he continues his reading, he sits down on the couch.*) "Dear Diary, since you and I are going to be great friends, I will start by telling you about myself. My name is Anne Frank. I am thirteen years old. I was born in Germany the twelfth of June, nineteen twenty-nine. As my family is Jewish, we emigrated to Holland when Hitler came to power." **B**

---

12. **bitter:** unaccepting.

In-Text Help

For another example, *The Holt Reader, Adapted Version, Second Course* includes two scenes from a play, *The Diary of Anne Frank*. To help students understand the dialogue, summaries titled In Other Words are provided at the bottom of each page.

After Reading the Selection

Skills Practice

For some selections, graphic organizers reinforce the skills students have practiced throughout the selection.

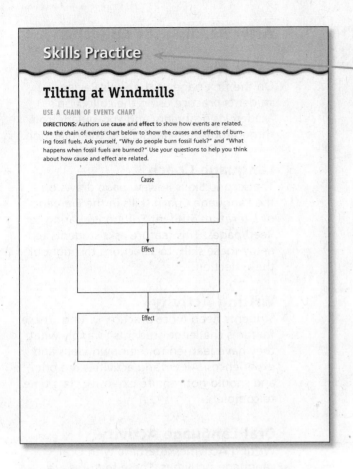

Skills Practice

Tilting at Windmills

USE A CHAIN OF EVENTS CHART

DIRECTIONS: Authors use **cause** and **effect** to show how events are related. Use the chain of events chart below to show the causes and effects of burning fossil fuels. Ask yourself, "Why do people burn fossil fuels?" and "What happens when fossil fuels are burned?" Use your questions to help you think about how cause and effect are related.

Cause

Effect

Effect

Applying Your Skills

This feature provides additional practice with selection vocabulary and literary, reading, and informational text focus skills. Some short selections will share a single Applying Your Skills page.

Applying Your Skills

Borders of Baseball: U.S. and Cuban Play

COMPREHENSION WRAP-UP

1. Consider what we have learned about Cuba and what we know about living in America. How well would we fit into the Cuban way of life?
2. Discuss the notion of pride. How is baseball in Cuba related to national pride?

INFORMATIONAL TEXT FOCUS: COMPARISON AND CONTRAST

DIRECTIONS: Circle the letter that best answers the question.

1. The method this writer uses for **comparing** and **contrasting** is the
   A. chronological method.   B. point-by-point method.
   C. persuasive method.   D. block method.

DIRECTIONS: Compare and **contrast** by filling in the following diagram. In each circle, write the differences between Cuban and American baseball. In the center, where the circles overlap, write the similarities.

Baseball in the U.S.   Baseball in Cuba

Differences   Similarities   Differences

VOCABULARY REVIEW

DIRECTIONS: Fill in the blanks with the correct words from the Word Box. Not all words will be used.

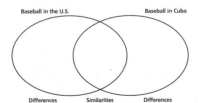

Word Box

compete
professionals
talented

1. Most players who are now _____ began playing baseball as children.
2. Many players will _____ to see who will be the most successful.

After Reading the Collection

Skills Review

Collection 3

LANGUAGE COACH: SLANG

Slang is informal, or casual, language that includes some newly invented words and some familiar words that have different meanings. For example, in the story "The War of the Wall," the character named Side Pocket asks "Watcha got there?" This is slang for "What do you have there?"

DIRECTIONS: Write what you think each slang sentence below means in more formal, or literary, language.

1. What's up? _____

2. Get a whiff of the exhaust from that truck! _____
_____

3. Whaddya think about that? _____

4. Lemme see! _____

WRITING ACTIVITY

DIRECTIONS: Does the writer of "Border of Baseball" present a balanced view of baseball in the United States and in Cuba? Write three or four sentences explaining why you think the writer does or does not present a balanced view **comparing** and **contrasting** baseball in the two countries.

_____
_____
_____
_____
_____

Skills Review
On the first page of the Skills Review, students practice using the collection's academic vocabulary and vocabulary from throughout the selections in the collection.

Language Coach
The second Skills Review page draws on the Language Coach skills in the *Elements of Literature* Student Edition Preparing to Read pages. This feature asks students to apply those skills to selections throughout the collection.

Writing Activity
Students need more practice writing. These features challenge students to apply what they have learned to their own ideas and experiences. All writing activities are brief, and should not require extensive class time to complete.

Oral Language Activity
Writing Activities alternate with Oral Language Activities. These features are designed to help students express their thoughts cogently in oral form. The features are particularly appropriate for students learning English or native speakers who need practice with Standard English.

Introductory Course

Collection 1

LA BAMBA

Major Understanding for Read and Discuss Queries: *In "La Bamba," Manuel learns what it takes to fulfill his dream of being in the limelight (and the consequences of taking that risk) and getting everyone's attention, including his family's.*

Page 3
A Read and Discuss
To establish that because Manuel is one of many children in his family and looks similar to most of the kids in his neighborhood—only average—he longs for attention and agrees to be in the school talent show even though he questions that decision: **What is the author letting us know about Manuel?** Possible response: He seems to want attention—maybe because he wants to impress his friends and Petra Lopez.

Page 4
C Language Coach
Possible answers: "flash"/ "shadow"/ "gravity"

Page 6
A Reading Focus
Possible answer: Students might predict that Manuel's performance will not continue to go well. Because the record player jammed during rehearsal, it seems likely that more problems could arise.

Page 7
B Vocabulary
This *cast* just performed at a talent show.

C Read and Discuss

To note that although Manuel thought his performance was embarrassing and horrible, the audience loved him: **How does everyone react to Manuel's performance?** Possible response: When the record skips, people laugh and get excited, but Manuel misinterprets their reaction as negative instead of positive. **Follow-up: What is all this about applause shaking the walls of the cafeteria?** Possible response: When Manuel comes out during the curtain call, the audience goes nuts for him.

D Literary Focus
Possible answer: Manuel's conflict is finally resolved when he realizes that everyone enjoyed his performance.

Comprehension Wrap-Up
1. Possible answer: The story shows us to face our fears, and never be afraid to try something that we want to do. One way or another, things will work out in the end.

Page 8
Skills Practice
Use a Concept Map
Possible answers:
1. Manuel feels nervous about performing in the talent show.
2. The record player jams during Manuel's rehearsal.
3. When Manuel first begins his act, the audience does not seem very excited.
4. During the talent show, the record player jams and Manuel has to mouth the chorus repeatedly.

Page 9
Applying Your Skills
Literary Focus
1. The climax is when Manuel performs in the talent show and the record player jams.
2. The resolution comes after Manuel's performance. When it is over, it is clear that everyone loved Manuel's performance and he suddenly becomes popular.

Reading Focus
1. No   2. Yes   3. No

Vocabulary Review
Students' answers will vary but should demonstrate an understanding of the word *cast* as it is used in this story.

THE GOLD CADILLAC

Major Understanding for Read and Discuss Queries: 'lois learns hard lessons about racism as her family travels from their home in the north to their grandmother's in Mississippi. 'lois and her father also learn that flashiness and attention brought on by material things isn't always worth it.

Page 12
B Read and Discuss
To set up the flurry of excitement surrounding the narrator's father's new purchase: **What has the author set up for us for far?** Possible response: The narrator and her sister are ecstatic at the sight of their new Cadillac—the one their father bought.

C Vocabulary
Here, *features* means "luxuries" or "components"

Page 13
D Reading Focus
To establish that 'lois's father seems to dote on his girls: **What does this scene shown us about the relationship between the sisters and their father?** Possible response: They seem to have a warm relationship—their father seems to like to make them happy.

Page 14
A Literary Focus
Possible answer: If this were a novel, the author would probably describe the car and the family's reaction in more depth. Because novellas are shorter than novels, the author has to be more concise here.

Page 15
C Read and Discuss
To further establish the depth of Dee's dissatisfaction with the purchase of the Cadillac: **What does it mean that "I could see from my mother's face she had not come around"?** Possible response: Even after the girls and their father were gone a long time, Dee is still angry about the car.

E Reading Focus
Students' predictions will vary, but may indicate that 'lois's father will eventually sell the Cadillac after hearing Dee's argument.

Page 16
A Read and Discuss
To draw attention to the reason Dee is so upset with the purchase of the Cadillac and to shed further light on Dee and the father's characters: **What does this part of the story show us about Dee's anger toward the Cadillac purchase?** Possible response: She sees the car as an obstacle to their larger goal of buying a house in a better neighborhood. **Follow-up: What does this purchase show us about 'lois's father and what does Dee's concern show us about her?** Possible Response: 'lois's father seems a little reckless and wild to buy an expensive car when they don't even need a new one. Dee's concern shows us how focused she is on moving their family toward their goals—she's conservative.

B Reading Focus
Possible answer: Because Sunday afternoon drives are important to the family, the Cadillac will likely be important, also.

C Reading Focus
Students' predictions will vary but might indicate that Dee will eventually agree to ride in the Cadillac and the family will go on a trip together.

Page 17
D Vocabulary
Possible answer: Something that is *evident* can be supported with *evidence*, or clear facts.

E Read and Discuss
To highlight the lengths Dee will go to illustrate her disgust with the Cadillac and that 'lois's father is sad about her reaction to the car: **How have these scenes added to what we know about 'lois's father and mother?** Possible Response: Dee is extremely stubborn. She still won't ride in it and won't let the girls ride in it to church. 'lois's father is a little down about Dee's absence at family events.

Page 18
A Literary Focus
Possible answer: If this were a short story, lines 201-203 would likely be cut altogether.

Because short stories are shorter than novellas, authors cannot be as wordy when writing short stories.

Page 19
B Vocabulary
Possible answer: 'lois' neighborhood must be safer than the South.

D Reading Focus
Students' answers will vary depending on their earlier predictions.

E Read and Discuss
To begin to develop the complicated nature of racism and how it figures in to 'lois's father driving the wonderful Cadillac into Mississippi: **What does the conversation between 'lois's father and his relatives show us about their life?** Possible response: It shows that although 'lois's father had the means to buy such a fancy car, driving it into Mississippi would have been viewed as an act of aggression by the whites who lived there.

Page 21
B Read and Discuss
To recognize 'lois's excitement about the trip and to begin to recognize that she doesn't understand the ramifications of them driving the Cadillac into the south: **What is 'lois thinking about the trip?** Possible response: She's thrilled about the grand picnic they're headed on, but is angry that her mother is still not impressed with the car and not happy to be on the trip.

Page 22
B Read and Discuss
To establish that 'lois finally understands the gravity of their trip through the south: **What does 'lois now understand about the real reason for the picnic?** Possible response: She finally understands that the reason her family packed the giant picnic is that they pass through states where there are no restaurants that allow blacks to eat in them. **Follow-up: Knowing what we do about 'lois, how must this information be sitting with her?** Possible Response: It must be devastating to learn that she can't do certain things simply because of her skin color.

C Reading Focus
Students' predictions will vary but may indicate that the policeman will treat 'lois's

dad badly. The policeman is already calling him "boy" and hinting that the Cadillac is not his.

Page 24
A Vocabulary
Possible answers: "Sunset"/ "evening"/ "late"/ "afternoon"/ twilight

B Reading Focus
Students' predictions will vary but may indicate that 'lois will understand why her mother dislikes the Cadillac.

Page 25
C Read and Discuss
To recognize that Wilbert finally grasps the gravity of driving such an extravagant car into the South: **What is going on?** Possible response: 'lois's father has decided it's too risky to drive any further in the Cadillac. He drives the car back to Memphis to exchange it with his cousin's Chevy. **Follow-up: What leads 'lois's father to this decision?** Possible response: Seeing 'lois asleep with a knife must have made him realize how much he is making his family suffer by driving the fancy car.

Page 27
B Reading Focus
Students' predictions will vary but may indicate that 'lois's father is shining the car so that he can exchange it for the family's old car.

Page 28
A Vocabulary
Ragged means "worn out" or "old."

Page 29
Comprehension Wrap-Up
Possible responses:
1. The Cadillac received lots of positive feedback from 'lois's family and friends. In the South, however, the racist police officers assumed that 'lois's father had stolen the Cadillac.
2. 'lois was surprised to see the signs of segregation in the South. She also had trouble understanding the police officers' suspicions of her father. It was probably her first encounter with so much racism.

Holt Adapted Reader Answer Key

Page 30
Skills Practice
Use a Prediction Chart
Students' answers will vary depending on their predictions, but should reflect students' understanding of the story.

Page 31
Applying Your Skills
Literary Focus
Possible answers:
1. 'lois's father buys a Cadillac; her mother opposes the decision.
2. 'lois's father takes the family in the Cadillac to Mississippi.
3. Two racist white policemen stop and harass them and put the father in jail for a few hours for no reason.
4. The family heads back north to borrow Cousin Halton's car to finish the drive to Mississippi.
5. 'lois's father sells the Cadillac after they get home.

Reading Focus
Possible answers:
1. I predict my car will break down soon.
2. I predict there will be a thunderstorm.

Vocabulary Review
1. ignorance   2. rural
3. evident

MAKING IT UP AS WE GO

Major Understanding for Read and Discuss Queries: After reading this historical piece, students should have an understanding of the different types of communication that have been used throughout the years and the problems that occur with some of them.

Page 34
B Read and Discuss
To establish that a young girl stumbled across an early form of communication while exploring in a cave: **What has the author told us in this first section?** Possible response: A young girl stumbled across some pictures and symbols while exploring a cave on her family's land. **Follow up: What's the significance of her findings?** Possible

response: We can't know for sure, but they may be a form of communication.

D Vocabulary
Possible answer: Writing is considered a *recent* invention because people communicated only by speaking for a long time before they started writing things down.

Page 35
E Read and Discuss
To reinforce the point being made by all of these facts – writing is a relatively new form of communication: **The author has given us a number of facts here. What is the point of this information?** Possible response: Considering the number of years human beings have been around, writing is relatively new. **Follow up: What is the author telling us about languages and writing?** Possible response: Although there are a lot of languages, even today, not all of them have a written form.

Page 36
B Reading Focus
Possible answer: Headings like this one help give the article structure and hint at what's coming in the paragraphs to follow.

C Reading Focus
Circle: "American tall tales, like those about Paul Bunyan and Babe the Blue Ox (the subjects of this California sculpture) are examples of stories spread by word of mouth."

Page 37
Applying Your Skills
Comprehension Wrap-Up
1. Possible response: We use sign language to communicate. Art can be used to communicate feelings and ideas. Morse code is another method of communication.

Informational Text Focus
Students' answers will vary considerably but students should demonstrate an understanding of how titles, subtitles, and headings help organize a story.

Vocabulary Review
1. permanent   2. Prehistoric
3. intriguing

IRAQI TREASURES HUNTED

Major Understanding for Read and Discuss Queries: This article illustrates the dramatic loss of valuable art and priceless objects from the Iraqi National Museum and archeological dig sites. The missing objects are far more valuable than any price put on them as they offer snapshots into the world's first civilizations.

Page 40
D Read and Discuss
To develop the degree to which early Mesopotamians were intelligent and inventive: **What do the inventions of people in Mesopotamia tell us about early civilization there?** Possible response: The Mesopotamians who lived so long ago were inventing and developing things that we still use today. That shows how smart they were. **Follow-up: How does this list of inventions add to our understanding of the importance of the missing objects?** Possible response: This list demonstrates the kinds of things the Mesopotamians were doing in everyday life and that makes us see how important their creations were to those who came after them and how important it is that the world maintain a collection of Mesopotamian items.

Page 41
E Reading Focus
Possible answer: This information is in a sidebar because it provides extra facts about ancient artifacts that have been recovered or that are still missing. The information here is set up us a list of different items, and that kind of structure fits well into a sidebar.

Page 42
A Vocabulary
police

D Read and Discuss
To establish that the looting of undocumented archeological digs is creating an even bigger problem than the looting of documented items housed in the National Museum: **Why have Iraqi officials made it against the law to remove objects from dig sites without permission?** Possible response: Dig sites aren't fully documented and many objects aren't even above the ground, so it's easy for thieves to take the items. Iraqi officials made a law against this to prevent such thievery.

Page 43
Applying Your Skills
Comprehension Wrap-Up
1. Possible response: These Iraqi artifacts provide us with a better understanding of world history since Mesopotamia is known as the birthplace of civilization. These artifacts are not just part of Iraq's history, but they belong to the whole world.

Informational Text Focus
Circle:
1. C   2. C   3. B

Vocabulary Review
1. authorities   2. recovered
3. civilizations

CAVE ONLINE

Major Understanding for Read and Discuss Queries: This short web article illustrates the surprising role of technology in the world of prehistoric art. Benjamin Britton's development of software has resulted in the ability for people to experience Lascaux Cave without having to enter the cave. This is a tremendous development as simply entering the cave and breathing causes the work to further deteriorate.

Page 45
B Read and Discuss
To establish that a group of artists are using technology to copy and capture the original, dramatic details of a work of art created on the walls of Lascaux cave 17,000 years ago: **How does technology fit into the world of prehistoric art?** Possible response: Technological advances have made it possible for a group of artists to copy a specific, ancient piece of cave art. The result the technology gives is good enough to create a traveling exhibit that would be worth seeing even though it is not the real thing.

C Reading Focus
Students should circle the table of contents along the left side of the page. Other articles: Fungus Among Us: A Dangerous Intruder, News Board, Education, and Ask the Digger.

Page 46
C Vocabulary
Possible answer: An artist's *talents* may include great painting and sculpting skills.

Page 47
E Reading Focus
Students should circle the "Related Links" box along the left side of the page.

Page 48
Skills Practice
Use a Web Site Table
Students' answers will vary considerably, but students must follow the provided steps. Answers should also reflect an understanding of the structural features of a Web site.

Page 49
Applying Your Skills
Comprehension Wrap-Up
1. Possible response: The two are so far removed that it does not seem likely for them to be related at all.

Informational Text Focus
1. C   2. B   3. C

Vocabulary Development
1. vivid   2. techniques

SKILLS REVIEW

Page 50
Vocabulary Review
1. b   2. d
3. c   4. b

Students' original sentences will vary but should demonstrate an understanding of the vocabulary words.

Page 51
Language Coach
Circle: "making"/ "ancient"/ "paintings"/ "cave"/ "laser"

Oral Language Activity
Students' answers will vary, but students should tell their partners stories they know from reading, TV, family members, or other places. Once they have practiced telling their stories in pairs, students should share with the entire class.

Collection 2

ALL SUMMER IN A DAY

Major Understanding for Read and Discuss Queries: This is a science fiction selection about astronauts' children living on Venus where there is sunshine once every seven years for only a two hour duration. Margot's classmates cruelly deprive her of that precious sunshine because of their jealousy and feelings that Margot is different and doesn't fit in with them.

Page 55
A Read and Discuss
To establish the setting in a classroom on the rainy planet Venus: **So how are things starting off?** Possible response: There's been seven years of continual rain for these students who are children of astronauts living on Venus with their families.

Page 56
B Read and Discuss
To emphasize that the rain is stopping and the children have no previous experience with the sun: **What are we learning from this part?** Possible response: The children have had to study about the sun because they have no recollection of sun; it last appeared when they were only two years old.

Page 57
D Literary Focus
Students' answers will vary, but opinions should reflect an understanding of William and Margot's relationship in the story.

Page 58
B Vocabulary
Vital means "necessary to live."

C Read and Discuss
To focus on how Margot differs from her classmates: **What is going on with Margot?** Possible response: Margot remembers the sun because she hasn't been on Venus as long as the other children and she's taunted and/or ignored by them, seems depressed, and keeps her distance from her classmates. There's been talk that Margot will return to earth within a year. **Follow up: How do William's comments connect to what we read earlier?**

Possible response: He's still taunting Margot because she doesn't join in with student games and songs like the others and because she remembers the sun while the others do not.

Page 59
E Reading Focus
Students' answers will vary, but should include the following details:
1. William tells Margot that the sun isn't coming out today.
2. The other children play along, pretending that they had been playing a joke on Margot all along.
3. Margot begins crying and the children lock her in a closet.

F Vocabulary
Surged means "swarmed around; rushed toward."

G Read and Discuss
To underscore the horror that Margot's classmates have isolated her from the sun: **What picture is the author creating for us?** Possible response: With one boy instigating, Margot is fighting, pleading, and crying as the students lock her in a closet away from the day that is to be sunny. The children smile and walk away as the teacher returns.

H Read and Discuss
How do the children seem to feel about what they have done to Margot? Possible response: The children do not care about Margot and her longing for the sun.

Page 60
A Literary Focus
Students' answers will vary, but should indicate that the sun has come out, and Margot is still trapped in the closet while the other children are outside.

B Language Coach
Possible answer: The dialogue allows the reader to better understand the children's excitement.

C Read and Discuss
To understand the children's delight with their first experience playing in the sunshine: **What has occurred here?** Possible response: The teacher returns and, without knowing about Margot, who's locked in the closet, takes the students outdoors to play in the sunshine.

Page 61
D Vocabulary
Savored means "delighted in; enjoyed thoroughly."

E Reading Focus
Answers will vary, but should include the following details:
1. The children ran and played in the sunlight.
2. One girl caught a drop of rain in her hand and began crying.
3. The rain began falling more heavily, as the children sadly headed back to their classroom.

F Read and Discuss
What has happened here? Possible response: It has started raining again. The children are upset.

Page 62
A Literary Focus
The children realized that Margot was locked in the closet for the entire length of time that it stopped raining.

B Read and Discuss
To understand the enormity of the children's cruelty to Margot: **What does this say about the students?** Possible response: They seemed to have completely forgotten about Margot in the midst of all the fun they were having in the sun. Perhaps now they can understand why, because of her memories of the sun, the sunshine has more significance for Margot. William took away from Margot what she most needed and wanted, so this is no simple prank. **Follow up: Remembering what we learned about Margot earlier, how might these new details impact her?** Possible response: She was so withdrawn before being locked away from the sun, now her utter silence may signal that she's completely broken emotionally and may need to return to earth soon.

Page 63
Applying Your Skills
Comprehension Wrap-Up
Possible responses:
1. Communication and understanding are important to human existence. Terrible things happen when people don't show compassion and care towards others.

Holt Adapted Reader Answer Key

2. The children are mean to Margot because they see her as different. They do not understand her, and people sometimes show disdain towards what they do not understand.

Literary Focus

1. Students' answers will vary, but should explain how being on Venus affects Margot's situation.

2. Students' answers will vary, but should reflect an understanding of how the other children's behavior helps shape the plot.

Reading Focus

Possible answers, as told from Margot's point of view:

1. I was excited at school this morning because the scientists said that the sun would come out today for a few hours.

2. We studied the sun in class and wrote poems about it, but the other students teased me and claimed that I did not remember what the sun is like.

3. While the teacher was out of the room, a boy named William began teasing and pushing me. Then he said that the sun was not really coming out today. The other children agreed with them.

4. William and the children then locked me in a closet. When they returned a few hours later to let me out, they all looked terrified.

Vocabulary Review

1. consequence **2.** surged
3. frail

WARTIME MISTAKES, PEACETIME APOLOGIES

Major Understanding for Read and Discuss Queries: After 48 years, Yoshiko Imamoto received compensation for the results of President Franklin Roosevelt's Executive Order 9066. She was one of more than 120,000 people of Japanese ancestry who were taken from their homes and jobs and transplanted into prison-like camps. In the case of Yoshiko and many others, a measure of justice took a lifetime.

Page 65
B Read and Discuss

To establish the motivation for President Franklin Roosevelt's Executive Order 9066 and successive presidents' involvement: **What did we learn about President Roosevelt's war order?** Possible response: In 1942 after Japan bombed Pearl Harbor, President Franklin Roosevelt put this plan into effect and Japanese Americans lost their homes and jobs when they were forced to leave and be warehoused in camps.

Page 66
A Reading Focus

Circle: "March 1942"/ "1945"/ "1990"

Comprehension Wrap-Up

1. Possible response: President Carter meant that if people were more accepting, political leaders could solve problems peacefully and without violating citizens' rights.

WHAT A CHARACTER: IWAO TAKAMOTO AND HIS TOONS

Major Understanding for Read and Discuss Queries: This story illustrates the boundless creativity of Iwao Takamoto and the way he seemed to make the life he wanted even with enormous obstacles in the way.

Page 68
B Read and Discuss

To set up that the author is going to illustrate the way two disparate things are intertwined through the life of one man: **What has the author set up for us?** Possible response: The author is going to explain how Iwao Takamoto came to create Scooby Doo after spending time in an internment camp. **Follow-up: Why would these two pieces of information be worthy of writing about?** Possible response: An internment camp must have been a horrible place to be, yet a person who lived in one ended up creating a famous cartoon. It's an interesting contrast.

Page 69
E Read and Discuss

To elicit the degree to which Takamoto's life has changed and to draw attention to his prolific artistic abilities: **What is going on?** Possible response: Takamoto left his job picking fruit to work for Disney, where he had great success. **What does the number of**

Holt Adapted Reader Answer Key

sketches he did before his initial Disney interview and his subsequent body of work let us know about the kind of professional Takamoto was? Possible response: He was very talented and hard working. He seemed to be able to work very fast and turn out exceptional work at the same time.

Page 70
A Read and Discuss
To establish Takamoto's ability to put an unexpected cartoon twist on real-life expectations: **How did Takamoto go about creating characters like Scooby Doo?** Possible response: Takamoto took what he saw in the world and made little changes that made his characters funnier than they might have been had he drawn them true to life. **Follow-up: What does this show us about Takamoto?** Possible Response: It shows the depth of his creativity, the ability to see things a little differently than the rest of us might.

B Reading Focus
Students' outlines will vary, but should include the following main ideas:
  I. Takamoto led a hard life during his internment, but he was encouraged by fellow inmates to keep up his drawing.
  a). After internment, he got a job as an animator with Disney.
  b). He also went on to work for Hanna-Barbera, succeeding there as well.
  II. Takamoto was very skilled at drawing lovable cartoon characters, becoming most famous for his dogs.
  a). He has been honored by many throughout his lifetime, and his work lives on.

Comprehension Wrap-Up
Possible responses:
  1. Takamoto might not have met those people who had worked in the movies and he might never have been encouraged to draw.
  2. Takamoto's heart was in his drawings, as he loved and cared for them, and that will continue to show in his work as time goes on.

Page 71
Applying Your Skills
Informational Text Focus
Possible answers:
Wartime Mistakes:

Detail 1: They were placed in camps due to an order from President Roosevelt.
Detail 2: America finally apologized decades later to those put in camps during WWII.
What a Character:
Detail 1: He created many famous cartoon characters, including Scooby Doo.
Detail 2: Takamoto is appreciated as one of the greatest animators of our time.

Vocabulary Review
  1. character   2. citizens
  3. animators   4. internment

SKILLS REVIEW

Page 72
Applying Your Skills
Vocabulary Review
  1. future   2. internment
  3. animators
Second part:
  1. The children were nine years old.
  2. Possible answers: She was put in a prison camp; She received a twenty-thousand dollar check and an apology note fifty years after the war.
  3. Possible answers: getting a job at Disney Studios, working on well-known Disney movies, working on well-known Hanna-Barbera cartoons, creating famous cartoon dogs, winning the Windsor McKay Lifetime Achievement Award, being honored by the Japanese American National Museum.

Page 73
Language Coach
Students' answers will vary, but should attempt to imitate Bradbury's use of strong and exciting vocabulary.

Writing Activity
Possible answers:
  1. "All Summer in a Day," by Ray Bradbury, takes place on Venus.
  2. Margot is the main character and wants to see the sun again; students should also explain the similarities and differences between Margot and the other important characters they mention.
  3. Margot can't see the sun because it is always raining. Just before the rain finally

stops, Margot's classmates lock her in a
closet and she misses the sun.

4. The period when the rain stops is the
climax of the story.

Collection 3

THE KING OF MAZY MAY

*Major understanding for Read and Discuss
Queries: This is Jack London's suspenseful
tale of a boy who battles to record a
neighbor's rich claim. In his part of the
world—the wild Yukon—young Walt restores
justice and makes a name for himself, the King
of Mazy May.*

Page 77
C Literary Focus
Possible answers: "strong"/ "brave"/ "not
afraid"/ "growing up"

D Read and Discuss
*To establish the rugged, youthful character of
Walt as he works with his father and to sense
that something unjust is brewing around them:*
What is the author setting up for us?
Possible response: Walt Masters is a strong,
good-hearted boy who is unsophisticated but
wise in the ways of the wilderness. He and his
father have moved to the Klondike and work
hard together on their claim. **Follow-up:
What seems to be the problem?** Possible
response: Walt, his dad, and some men have
been successful. Some greedy men want to
cash in on people's success and steal their
claims.

Page 78
B Read and Discuss
*To discern Walt's mission to help Loren Hall
and his motivation:* **What is going on with
Walt here?** Possible response: Walt is
sparked into action so that old Loren Hall's
claim gets recorded—then the land and what's
mined on it will legally belong to Mr. Hall.
Because it's so much quicker and easier to
take what someone else has discovered,
there's a long history in the Yukon of stealing
what rightfully belongs to others. **Follow-up:
Why doesn't Loren record his claim like
Walt's dad did?** Possible response: Loren is
an old prospector who has no dogs to speed

his travel to Dawson to record his claim. In
addition, due to an injury, Loren can't leave
now.

C Reading Focus
Possible answers: circle: "crept carefully"/
"built a fire"/ "frozen gravel"/ "melt the ice in
gold pans"

D Vocabulary
Harnessed means "fastened" or "brought
under control."

Page 79
E Read and Discuss
*To recognize that Walt's kind-hearted decision
to help Loren Hall means there's difficulty
ahead for Walt:* **What does Walt's plan here
tell us about what kind of person he is?**
Possible response: This shows Walt's good
heart as he plans to drive dogs to Dawson in
order to establish Loren Hall's claim since the
old man cannot now do it on his own. Walt is
taking on a tough task as the trek is long and
Walt is chased by furious claim-jumpers who
must know that Walt has figured out what they
are up to.

F Read and Discuss
*To appreciate the developing suspense as
young Walt continues on his journey to
Dawson:* **What is all this saying about
Walt's trip?** Possible response: This is
suspenseful! The two claim-jumpers in a dog
sled are chasing Walt and shooting at him
along the winding trail.

Page 80
C Reading Focus
Students' answers will vary, but should
recognize that the author does a good job of
showing the action to the reader by providing
intense detail and strong word choices.

Page 81
D Read and Discuss
*To acknowledge Walt's stamina and
resourcefulness along the trek and to
understand the reason for calling Walt the
King of Mazy May:* **How does the author end
the story?** Possible response: As Walt realizes
he needs to change the lead dog, the claim-
jumpers' shots hit that dog! Walt cuts the dog
free, holds off the men who have caught up
with him and tips their sled over. With a better
lead dog now and the men occupied with

Holt Adapted Reader Answer Key

righting their sled, Walt races ahead of the men to Loren Hall's camp, alerts him to the problems and both pull into Dawson to record Loren's rightful claim to his gold. **Follow-up: Why is Walt now called the "King of Mazy May"?** To honor the boy's struggle, men called Walt the King of Mazy May—Mazy May being the name of the local creek.

Comprehension Wrap-Up
Possible responses:

1. With great detail and diction, London creates suspense and action, such as when he describes one of the men leaping over snowbanks with "the quickness of a cat" to chase after Walt, and with phrases like "bullets singing after him."

2. The author introduces Walt by showing what he is not; then he shows how fearless and heroic Walt is by describing the dangerous actions Walt takes in order to stop the bad men.

Page 82
Skills Practice
Use a Word Web
Possible answers:

1. He is intelligent.
2. He is resourceful.
3. He drives a dog sled.
4. He lives with just his father in the Yukon because his mother passed away.

Page 83
Applying Your Skills
Literary Focus

1. Possible answer: The Klondike area of the Yukon Territory is very dangerous, especially during a high-speed chase, making the story more exciting.
2. Possible answer: The story would be completely different if it were set in the desert. Teams of dogs are not used for traveling over sand. The author would probably have chosen a different resource around which to center the story.

Reading Focus
Students' answers and sketches will vary, but should depict a young, tough boy.

Vocabulary Review
1. moccasins **2.** gravel

OLYMPIC GLORY: VICTORIES IN HISTORY

Major Understanding for Read and Discuss Queries: The students should understand that the selection compares and contrasts ancient Olympic Games and athletes with those of modern times.

Page 85
A Read and Discuss
To establish some similarities between the original Greek Olympics and the present-day version: **What point is the author trying to make in the first two paragraphs?** Possible response: From the earliest to the modern Olympics, there are similarities and differences concerning events and athletes. **Follow-up: What features of the Olympics remain the same across time?** Possible response: Similarities are the thrill of victory for spectators and athletes alike. Likewise, the athletes represent their homelands and their skills.

B Reading Focus
Possible answers: Similarities: The glory, the crowds, the patriotic feelings. Differences: Instead of athletes just being from Greece like in the ancient Games, athletes who compete in the modern Games come from all over the world. Also, the host cities for the modern Games are not located only in Greece.

Page 86
C Read and Discuss
To reinforce additional similarities between ancient and modern Olympians: **What is the author letting us know about an Olympic athlete?** Possible response: Olympians— ancient or modern, male or female—are highly qualified and committed to their sport and compete for a prize and/or fame.

Page 87
D Vocabulary
A *ceremony* is "a formal act performed as a ritual or custom."

E Read and Discuss
To recognize that the Olympic torch and ceremony are a relatively new part of the Olympic festivities: **What is the author telling us about the Olympic torch?** Possible response: The Olympic torch ceremony only dates back to 1928, so it is a more recent development.

Holt Adapted Reader Answer Key

Comprehension Wrap-Up

1. Possible response: The author is comparing and contrasting ancient and modern Olympic Games—comparing by showing how things have remained the same, contrasting by showing how they have differed. When the author states that "some elements…stay the same," she means that there are still many similarities between the ancient Games and today's Games.

Page 88
Skills Practice
Use a Venn Diagram

Possible answers:
Ancient Olympics: The Games were part of a festival honoring Zeus; they were held in Olympia, Greece.
Same: The Games are held every four years; athletes compete for fame and pride.
Today's Olympics: Today the Olympics take place in the winter as well as the summer; the Olympic torch is a modern tradition.

Page 89
Applying Your Skills
Informational Text Focus

1. d   2. c and d

Vocabulary Review

1. ceremony
2. Possible answer: Athletes compete for Olympic pride and glory.
3. a
4. c

SKILLS REVIEW

Page 90
Vocabulary Review

1. False	6. False
2. False	7. True
3. False	8. False
4. False	9. False
5. False	10. True

Students' answers will vary, but should reflect an understanding of the meaning of *circumstances*.

Page 91
Language Coach

Students should put a check mark next to these words with multiple meanings:

1. general: (1) adj.; overall; customary, or (2) n.; a rank in the military
2. article: (1) n.; a newspaper story, or (2) n.; an item for sale
3. tie: (1) v.; to bind with rope or string, or (2) n.; a necktie
4. poor: (1) adj.; not having much money, or (2) adj.; not good in quality

Writing Activity

Students' answers will vary. Students should refer to their Venn diagrams to identify similarities and differences between the ancient Games and today's Games.

Collection 4

TA-NA-E-KA

Major Understanding for Read and Discuss Queries: Everyone in Mary's family learns that there are ways to incorporate new twists into old traditions. Most of all, Mary learns— through handling her quest her own way—that she loves and respects her tribe's traditions more than she ever realized.

Page 95
B Read and Discuss

To explore Mary and Roger's attitudes toward Ta-Na-E-Ka: **How does "Eleven" connect to Ta-Na-E-Ka?** Possible response: Age eleven—Mary and Roger's age—signifies a time when a child turns into an adult. Ta-Na-E-Ka means "flowering of adulthood" and is an endurance ritual each person must go through. **Follow-up: What do Roger and Mary think of Ta-Na-E-Ka?** Possible Response: It doesn't seem as though Roger and Mary appreciate the ritual and what it means to their family. They don't see the way their heritage fits with their ambitions to leave the reservation.

Page 96
C Read and Discuss

To draw attention to the Kaw's historical inclination toward men and women's equality: **How does women's liberation connect to the Kaw history and traditions?** Possible response: The Kaw are unusual in that they've always treated the women of the tribe equal to the men. Even their ancient legends illustrate the power of women and their position in Kaw society—revered and equal. **Follow-up: What does Mary think of this?** Possible Response: On one hand, it makes her upset because the notion of equality means she has to do Ta-Na-E-Ka like the boys. But mostly she's impressed with the way her tribe has treated women.

D Literary Focus
Students' answers may vary but might touch upon the passing down of one's heritage from generation to generation.

Page 97
E Vocabulary
Overslept means "slept longer than planned."

F Read and Discuss
To establish the connection between Mary's plan, the idea behind Ta-Na-E-Ka and what Grandfather would think of it: **Knowing what we do about Grandfather, what might he think of Mary's plan?** Possible response: He probably wouldn't like that she slept in the restaurant since it's a modern solution. He didn't even want the kids to be able to wear bathing suits for Ta-Na-E-Ka, let alone have a few meals at a restaurant and sleep inside it.

H Reading Focus
Possible answers: underline: "'It isn't silly…It's why the Kaw are great warriors'"/ "I'd never felt better,"/ "I watched the sun rise on the Missouri."

Page 98
B Read and Discuss
To determine that Roger and Mary had very different survival experiences: **How do things look for Mary and Roger?** Possible response: After a week on their own, Mary's physically much better off than Roger—clearly he survived the old fashioned way.

C Vocabulary
Possible answer: *Rotten* means "bad-tasting."

D Read and Discuss
To determine that although Grandfather has accepted Mary's handling of Ta-Na-E-Ka as a testament to her strength and survival skills, he's still not totally happy with the way she did it: **How have things wrapped up for**

Mary and Grandfather? Possible response: He's not thrilled with her execution of Ta-Na-E-Ka, but understands she has proven she can survive in the larger world, outside their family and tribe. He respects that.

Page 99
Applying Your Skills
Comprehension Wrap-Up
1. Possible response: Students should discuss Roger's toughing it out and Mary's milkshake and hamburger adventures.

Literary Focus
Students' answers will vary, but should indicate the difficulty of honoring both Indian heritage and modern day society.

Reading Focus
1. Yes   2. No   3. No
4. Yes   5. No

Vocabulary
1. overslept   2. rotten
3. refuse

THE DOG OF POMPEII

Major Understanding for Read and Discuss Queries: This is a story about a blind orphan boy and his constant companion, a resourceful, selfless dog named Bimbo who live in ancient Pompeii. When an earthquake overtakes Pompeii, the dog gallantly prods Tito through a crumbling city and out to the sea where the boy is rescued. The end of the story ties the past to present as archeologists find the remains of a dog with petrified raisin cake in its mouth, a food that Tito enjoyed.

Page 101
A Read and Discuss
To introduce the main characters Tito and Bimbo who live together in Pompeii: **What is the author letting us know about Bimbo the dog?** Possible response: Bimbo the dog is like a nurse, a parent, and a playmate to the blind boy named Tito. They live together in the ancient, busy city of Pompeii.

Page 102
A Vocabulary
A *forum* is a public square.

    Holt Adapted Reader Answer Key

B Reading Focus

Possible answer: People of ancient Pompeii didn't understand or agree on how the Earth worked.

C Read and Discuss

To draw attention to the speculation about why earthquakes occur: **What is going on at the forum?** Possible response: People are talking about earthquakes like the one that happened in Pompeii 12 years ago and everyone has a different opinion about why they occur.

D Literary Focus

Students' answers will vary but may indicate that these details make the characters more credible. These characters exist in a time when there was very limited knowledge on the subject of volcanoes.

Page 103
E Read and Discuss

To reiterate that the boy and dog are constant companions: **What is this telling us about Tito and Bimbo?** Tito is with Bimbo even at night when they go to an outdoor theatre performance. Blind Tito is attentive to the sounds around him and is thankful for his dog's quick instinct that keeps him out of harm's way.

Page 104
A Language Coach

These verbs are all in the past form, or tense.

B Reading Focus

Possible answers: Being near an erupting volcano must be a scary experience. As dust fills the air, it becomes harder to breath. The rocks and pebbles flying through the air must also be dangerous.

Page 105
D Read and Discuss

To highlight Tito's anguish in losing his companion, Bimbo: **If Tito was saved, why does it say, "no one could comfort him"?** Possible response: Tito realizes that his dog is no longer with him and that he is totally alone.

E Read and Discuss

To connect the past to the present in the story of Tito and his companion Bimbo: **What is this part about? The scientists are wondering why the dog would want a raisin cake at such a bad time. What strikes you**

about this? Possible response: This is about a modern day restoration of the forum section of Pompeii. Near a bakery, a dog's skeleton has been uncovered—a dog with a raisin cake in its mouth, the kind Bimbo got for Tito. **Follow up: The scientists are speculating about why the dog would want a raisin cake at such a precarious time. What strikes you about this?** Possible response: Perhaps as the text says earlier, the dog would regularly find food for both of them and keeps to that schedule despite the ensuing earthquake.

F Literary Focus

Students' answers will vary, but should reflect an understanding of credible characters.

Comprehension Wrap-Up

1. Possible response: Writing about ancient times must be difficult, because writers have to imagine what things were like. To have the best possible understanding of the ancient worlds, writers must do a lot of research.

Page 106
Skills Practice
Use a Character Evaluation Chart

Students' examples will vary, but should provide ample support for students' opinions and reflect an understanding of credibility.

Page 107
Applying Your Skills
Literary Focus

Students' opinions for questions 1 and 2 will vary, but should reflect an understanding of the story's events and the idea of credibility.

Reading Focus

Possible answers:
1. Without Bimbo, Tito will have a hard time surviving.
2. Bimbo is a very intelligent dog, and cares a lot for Tito.

Vocabulary Review

1. No   2. Yes   3. Yes

PET ADOPTION APPLICATION

Major Understanding for Read and Discuss Queries: This Pet Adoption Application demonstrates the seriousness with which organizations take the process of adopting a pet.

Page 109
B Reading Focus
Possible answer: A yard can provide a place for your adopted pet to get exercise and run around.

C Read and Discuss
To establish that officials are selective about who is allowed to adopt a pet: **What do the variety and number of questions on the form tell you about adopting a pet?** This application shows us that the people at this adoption organization delve deep into the lives of prospective owners. They must view adoption of an animal as an important event not to be undertaken lightly.

Page 110
Skills Practice
Use a Comparison Table
Possible answers:
1. If there are two people living in a home, the chances are greater that someone will be able to spend time with the pet.
2. If a person's work hours are just too long and he or she will not be able to spend much time with the animal, maybe having a pet isn't the best idea.
3. If a person has owned pets in the past, they have some experience with taking care of animals.

Page 111
Applying Your Skills
Comprehension Wrap-Up
1. Possible response: The agency would have to ensure that the person receiving the adopted pet as a gift would be a good owner.

Informational Text Focus
1. No, the application indicates that you can make a voluntary contribution, but there is no required fee.
2. No, references should be adults.
3. No, you should write "n/a" for a question that does not apply to you.
4. It is important to proofread the application to ensure that there are no mistakes.

Vocabulary Review
1. Yes   2. No   3. No

SKILLS REVIEW

Page 112
Vocabulary Review
Circle: "attitude"/ "refuse"/ "single"/ "occupation"

Page 113
Language Coach
1. a. smaller   b. smallest
2. a. lighter   b. lightest

Oral Language Activity
Students' debates will vary, but should reflect their understanding of the stories. Students must also use the terms "credible" and "theme" correctly.

Collection 5

FROM THE LAND I LOST

Major Understanding for Read and Discuss Queries: This is a humorous "tall tale" that the author remembers from his youth in Vietnam. It is about a remarkable bride who was more clever than the wily crocodile who snatched her. Although her husband never gave up in his search for her, the relatives were too frightened to help him because according to the old belief, the first victim would lure someone else to the crocodile.

Page 117
B Read and Discuss
To establish information about the author's childhood home in Vietnam: **What have we learned so far about the author and his childhood?** Possible response: Huynh Quang Nhuong grew up in Vietnam between a jungle and high mountains in an area so remote that there were no stores. There were, however, plenty of wild animals like crocodiles.

Page 118
A Read and Discuss
To emphasize that this part is one of the Vietnamese stories he heard long ago: **How does the author start the "So Close" section of this story?** Possible response: The author has a narrator introduce lots of characters and explains that Lan and Trung will marry.

B Literary Focus

Circle: "she"/ "her"

Page 119
E Vocabulary

Relatives are family members.

F Read and Discuss

To introduce the evil crocodile who has snatched the new bride: **Now what is happening with Lan and Trung?** Possible response: The crocodile grabs Lan when she goes to bathe in the river. Trung gets worried and goes to investigate, finding only her clothes left behind. **Follow-up: What are the relatives doing?** Possible response: Because they said they could not do anything to help, they went home.

G Reading Focus

Circle: "crying"/ "staring at his bride's clothes"

Page 120
A Language Coach

Possible answer: "bashed"

B Read and Discuss

To sort out the story of Lan's plan to escape the crocodile: **What is Lan explaining about her plan to get home?** Possible response: Lan fools the crocodile by playing dead, then climbs a tree when the crocodile is gone. She calls out to Trung to rescue her.

C Read and Discuss

To reinforce the joyous ending: **How does this story end?** Possible response: Lan is better in three days and the mothers are so glad to regain Lan that they plan a second wedding for their children.

Comprehension Wrap-Up

Possible responses:
1. The author feels that he "lost" Vietnam in the sense that everything changed after the war. But he will always remember the country's stories, and that brings him joy.
2. Thinking quickly is as important to our daily lives as it is to Lan. We must think quickly in many capacities—whether taking a test or improvising a line in a school play.

Page 121
Applying Your Skills
Literary Focus

Students' answers will vary. Students should correctly change lines 94 to 100 of the text from a first-person to a third-person. The pronoun *she*, for instance, should be *I* in students' answers.

Reading Focus

Students' answers will vary and should be supported with examples from the text.

Vocabulary Review
1. ancestors   2. altar
3. persuade

STORM

Major Understanding for Read and Discuss Queries: This story goes beyond the notion that a dog is man's best friend. It explores one special relationship shared by a man and his dog and the powerful ways in which they were able to communicate.

Page 123
B Read and Discuss

To establish the idea that this story is going to be about a dog named Storm and the lessons he was able to teach his owner: **What has the author told us so far about Storm?** Possible response: The narrator is talking about a dog named Storm and the important lessons he taught his owner.

Page 124
A Read and Discuss

To highlight Storm's personality: **What new information has the author given us about Storm?** Possible response: He is always playing tricks on the other dogs.

B Reading Focus

Possible answer: The author's purpose is to entertain his readers and inform them of Storm's quirks.

Page 125
D Read and Discuss

To reinforce the idea that Storm has a unique personality and to draw attention to the tricks that he played on his owner: **How does this new information add to what we already know about Storm?** *Not only did Storm play tricks on the other sled dogs, he also played tricks on his owner.* **Follow up: What does the owner think of the tricks Storm played** on him? Possible response: He actually thinks Storm enjoyed playing tricks, because he thinks he saw him smiling when he finally found his hat Storm buried.

E Literary Focus
Personification

Page 127
B Read and Discuss
To reinforce Storm's analytical nature: **What is going on with Storm?** Possible response: He was watching them put the stove on the sled, thinking intently about whether it would be too much weight.

C Reading Focus
Students' answers will vary, but any of the four possible purposes is acceptable as long as students back up their responses with evidence from the text.

D Literary Focus
Imagery

E Read and Discuss
To reinforce the idea that Storm has a "special" personality: **How does the fact that Storm became bored connect with what we already know about him?** Possible response: Storm is a special dog with human characteristics, so it would make sense that he became bored with the Iditarod training.

Page 128
A Literary Focus
A simile.

B Read and Discuss
To recognize that Storm solved his problem of boredom with the addition of a stick: **How does Storm solve his problem?** Possible response: He entertains himself with a stick. **Follow-up: What is the meaning of this stick?** Possible response: Storm sees the stick as a means of communication with his owner.

Page 129
Comprehension Wrap-Up
1. Possible response: In many ways, Storm was more of a friend to the narrator than a pet. He was able to entertain and communicate with his owner—those abilities made a special dog.

Page 130

Skills Practice
Use a Comparison Table
Students' answers will vary, but sentences should be relevant to "Storm" and correctly utilize the designated literary devices.

Page 131
Applying Your Skills
Literary Focus
1. Simile   2. Personification
3. Metaphor

Reading Focus
Possible answers:
1. To entertain, because Storm's pranks are funny to read about.
2. To express feelings, because it is touching that the narrator was so close to Storm.

Vocabulary Review
1. gratified   2. resembled   3. innocent

THE MYSTERIOUS MR. LINCOLN

Major Understanding for Read and Discuss Queries: This selection sites contradictions in Abraham Lincoln's complex character— humorous yet melancholy, sociable yet reticent, logical yet superstitious. He was considered to be a commoner yet in truth Lincoln had lucrative legal and investment careers. In his time, Lincoln was the most unpopular president, yet he's a folk hero today.

Page 134
A Read and Discuss
To establish Lincoln's appearance and the idea that there was more beneath the surface than what was conveyed: **What is the author telling us about Lincoln?** Possible response: Lincoln was tall and seemingly homely, but he'd come alive when talking with people and appear far more attractive when he was engaged with others. The long photo process of his day could not capture the real Lincoln's personality.

D Vocabulary
Folksy means "simple, "down-to-earth;" or "friendly."

E Read and Discuss
To sort out the authentic from the legendary versions of Lincoln: **What is this part about?**

Possible response: It is true that Lincoln appeared to be a common man, but unlike the ordinary citizen he had a prosperous legal career and had many investments. He was very ambitious and proud of his accomplishments.

Page 135
F Reading Focus
Possible answer: The author's purpose is to inform readers of other aspects of Lincoln's personality with which they may be unfamiliar.

G Literary Focus
The insult is a metaphor. Students should explain that this compares Lincoln, a human being, to an animal.

H Read and Discuss
To acknowledge the contradicting opinions about Lincoln: **How do Douglass's opinions of Lincoln in this part connect to this selection as a whole?** Possible response: Frederick Douglass, a black leader of Lincoln's time, was initially highly critical of Lincoln's leadership but later Douglass came to recognize and admire Lincoln's changing views as he advocated the end of slavery. Mr. Douglass had wildly opposing feelings about President Lincoln's depth of character and wisdom and those opposing facets of Lincoln's personality keep arising in the selection.

Comprehension Wrap-Up
1. Possible response: The selection's title echoes the reading's message—that Lincoln was an interesting individual who is often misunderstood.

Page 136
Skills Practice
Use a Comparison Table
Possible answers:
1. The author is trying to convince readers that pictures of Lincoln are misleading due to the low quality of photography at the time, so his purpose is to persuade us into changing our opinions of Lincoln.
2. The author's purpose in sharing these humorous facts about Lincoln is to entertain his readers.
3. In sentimentalizing Lincoln, the author is expressing his feelings about the "American folk hero."

Page 137
Applying Your Skills
Literary Focus
Students' answers will vary and are acceptable as long as they use the designated literary devices correctly and stay on topic.

Reading Focus
Students' answers will vary, but should be supported with evidence from the text.

Vocabulary Review
1. antonyms   2. synonyms
3. synonyms

WHAT DO FISH HAVE TO DO WITH ANYTHING?

Major Understanding for Read and Discuss Queries: This is a story of a sensitive, observant, inquisitive 5th grader whose divorced mother seems overprotective and reticent as he tries to stretch out into the world and learn about life. The man on the street tries to get Willie to think for himself.

Page 140
A Read and Discuss
To introduce the mother and son: **What do you think the author is telling us about Mrs. Markham and Willie?** Possible response: Mrs. Markham seems fussy when measuring out an exact portion of cake for Willie and he seems to mirror that behavior in the way he tidies up. We get the feeling that being smart and having money are important to both of them.

Page 141
C Reading Focus
Possible answer: The author's purpose is to express and examine the feelings that Willie has. Willie's asking about the homeless man is part of his growing up and learning to understand feelings like unhappiness.

Page 142
A Read and Discuss
To raise the issue of unhappiness and Willie's inquisitive manner: **What are Willie and his mother talking about here?** Possible response: Willie wonders about the homeless man's being unhappy and Mother says that money can cure a lot of unhappiness. Mother

seems troubled by some of Willie's questions or by her inability to answer them.

Page 143
B Read and Discuss
To emphasize Willie's observant manner:
What is Willie up to here? Possible response: He's noticing that no one gives the man money.

C Literary Focus
Symbolism

Page 144
A Literary Focus
Underline "The empty apartment felt like a cave that lay deep below the earth."

Page 145
D Read and Discuss
What does it say about Willie that he keeps thinking about the homeless man? Possible response: It shows that Willy is a curious and thoughtful boy.

E Language Coach
Possible answers: "depressed,"/ "melancholy"

F Read and Discuss
To recognize that Mom seems so closed and unseeing like a fish that lives in underwater caves and to raise the issue that perhaps she's fearful now that Dad's gone: **How do these conversations add to what we have already been thinking about Willie and his mother?** Mom still seems to be very protective, trying to shield Willie from the hurts of the world, and he, instead, wants to question and investigate life. He seems more honest and trusting than Mom. **Follow up: What is with the discussion about Dad?** Possible response: Mom says, "People are ashamed to be unhappy," and Willie personalizes that by responding, "Since Dad left, you've been unhappy. Are you ashamed?" In general, Willie's questions get to the heart of matters, but Mom regularly brushes him off.

G Reading Focus
Possible answers: The author's purpose here is to express feelings. We learn a lot about both Mother and Willie here. Mother leaves questions about her husband alone, and would rather not even think about them. Willie obviously cares for his Dad, and is concerned about how his father feels.

Page 146
A Read and Discuss
What was that about a fish? Willie learned about a type of fish that lived in caves so dark that it had no need of eyes.

Page 147
C Language Coach
Possible answers: "quiet"/ "noiseless"/ "hushed"

Page 148
B Read and Discuss
To establish that the begging man will be Willie's resource as he seeks a cure for unhappiness: **What is going on between the man and Willie?** Willie is trying to learn a cure for his Mom's unhappiness from the man.

Page 149
C Reading Focus
Possible answer: The author's purpose is to persuade his reader into thinking differently. The man on the street treats Willie like an adult, whereas Mrs. Markham belittles her son.

Page 150
A Read and Discuss
To understand that Willie can think for himself when cutting the cake: **What happened between the man and Willie?** Possible response: The two talk again, Willie offers him cake, and in his mother's exacting way, he measures the cake. The man objects to the portion requirement stated on the box saying that it's up to Willie to make the judgment on the size of the piece that he cuts.

B Language Coach
Possible answer: "never"

C Read and Discuss
To draw attention to the man's cure for unhappiness and Willie's response: **What did we learn here?** Possible response: Willie gave the man an inch and a half size piece of cake rather than his Mom's usual half inch piece. The man then gave what he had to offer, his cure for unhappiness—"What a person needs is always more than they say." **Follow-up: How does Willie respond to the man's answer?** Possible response: After hearing the cure, Willie offers his one and a half inch piece to the man and is complimented by the man.

Page 151
D Literary Focus

Possible answer: Yes, the blind fish can be viewed as a symbol for Willie's mother. She is unable to see Willie for who he really is. She is also blind to the roots of her own unhappiness.

Page 152
B Read and Discuss

To set up the conflict between Mom and her son: **What is the author letting us know here?** Possible response: Willie tells Mom about the cure for unhappiness. Mom says it's nonsense and that she's told the police that the man was bothering kids and so he's gone.

C Read and Discuss

To appreciate the underlying problem between Willie and Mom: **What are Willie and Mom trying to say to each other?** Possible response: He's trying to tell Mom that she's like the fish who lived deep under water and has lost its ability to see; she feels the man is a threat to Willie. Has she lost her ability to see because of the divorce? He's furious because he enjoyed talking with the man and Mom made him leave. Mom thinks Willie's got a vivid imagination and doesn't listen to all he says. Although both are trying to help each other, the messages are not getting through.

Page 153
Applying Your Skills
Comprehension Wrap-Up

1. Possible response: At the story's end, Mrs. Markham is oblivious to the analogy William is making when he calls her a fish. Mrs. Markham is also unhappy because she is more concerned about what "they" (others) think than with her own feelings.

Literary Focus

Students' answers will vary considerably. Possible simile: I was as hungry as a lion. Possible metaphor: My mom is a rock. Possible personification: The screaming wind whipped the kite.

Reading Focus

Possible answers:
1. To entertain and to express feelings. Storm's behavior is sometime funny, and reading about the dog's antics can be very entertaining. At the same time, the narrator has a very close, emotional connection with his dog, which the story clearly gets across.
2. To inform and to persuade. The author gives facts and information about Lincoln in order to give readers a clearer portrait of the former President. The author also tries to get readers to think about Lincoln in a new light.
3. To express feelings. The author shows us what's inside the characters in this story, from Willie's curiosity and concern to Mother's distancing from others.

Vocabulary Review
1. spare   2. begging

ALL ABOARD WITH THOMAS GARRETT

Major Understanding for Read and Discuss Queries: This story explores Thomas Garrett's role in the Underground Railroad and the sacrifices he made to help people who were so savagely oppressed. It illustrates the way a person's great generosity can have an impact on the lives of others—even if it takes decades.

Page 156
B Read and Discuss

To set up the risky business of helping runaway slaves to freedom: **What is the author showing us with Harriet Tubman and Thomas Garrett's actions?** Possible response: Their disguises and fast pace to the Pennsylvania border shows it was difficult to take a slave to freedom.

Page 157
C Vocabulary

Vowed means "promised."

Page 158
A Read and Discuss

To further establish Garrett's generosity and to discern that his passion shows others he is right: **How do things turn out in court?** Possible response: Garrett loses the case and owes money he can't begin to pay. **Follow-up: What does the juror's reaction to Garret's speech demonstrate?** Possible response: Garrett's passionate speech wins over people who in the past disagreed with him. The speech shows how persuasive Garrett can be.

B Reading Focus
Possible answer: The main idea is that Thomas Garrett opposed slavery and was willing to go to extreme lengths to support its abolition.

C Vocabulary
Here, *bands* means "groups of people."

Page 159
D Read and Discuss
To establish the degree to which black people admired Garrett: **What does this celebration show us?** Possible response: The celebration shows how much black people admired Garrett and the work he did to assist slaves in gaining their freedom.

Comprehension Wrap-Up
1. Possible response: A person must really believe in something to dedicate his or her life to that cause. For instance, Thomas Garrett truly believed in equality, so he was willing to endanger himself to free slaves.

Page 160
Skills Practice
Use an Organization Map
Possible answers:
1. For many years, Garrett broke the law by helping runaway slaves escape.
2. Garrett was not rich, but he used the little money he had to help escaping slaves.
3. Garrett worked with Harriet Tubman in helping slaves escape along the Underground Railroad.
4. After the abolition of slavery, former slaves celebrated Garrett as their "Moses."

Page 161
Applying Your Skills
Informational Text Focus
Students' paragraphs will vary, but their main ideas should reflect the details they compiled on the Skills Practice page.

SKILLS REVIEW
Page 166

Vocabulary Review
1. bands   2. elderly   3. vowed

FROM HARRIET TUBMAN: THE MOSES OF HER PEOPLE

Major Understanding for Read and Discuss Queries: This short piece offers another view into the dramatic and difficult journey Harriet took for the benefit of people who might not have attempted to run away without her assistance.

Page 164
A Read and Discuss
To recognize the strength of Harriet Tubman's character and commitment to her beliefs as she made the Underground Railroad a reality: **What do Harriet Tubman's actions tell you about her? Why would it take courage to do what she had done?** Possible response: Traveling the path of the Underground Railroad was grueling and to think Tubman did it so many times shows her strength and dedication to freeing other slaves.

C Reading Focus
Possible answer: underline: "But I was free, and they should be free also."

Comprehension Wrap-Up
1. Possible response: Many of the things Harriet Tubman did sound incredibly challenging. She carried on with them because she was so dedicated to eradicating slavery.

Page 165
Applying Your Skills
Informational Text Focus
Students' answers will vary, but should identify a common main idea in both Garrett's and Tubman's dedication to freeing slaves. Students should continue to support this main idea with examples from both texts.

Vocabulary Review
1. Yes   2. No
3. Yes   4. No

Vocabulary Review
1. d   5. g
2. c   6. h
3. b   7. f
4. a   8. e

Students' sentences will vary, but should reflect an understanding of the vocabulary words.

Page 167
Language Coach
1. Antonyms 2. Synonyms 3. Antonyms
4. Synonyms 5. Antonyms

Writing Language
Students' answers will vary, but should demonstrate an understanding of first-person point of view. Students should use words like "I," "me," and "mine" to make the passages first-person narratives.

Collection 6

A SURPRISING SECRET TO A LONG LIFE: STAY IN SCHOOL

Major Understanding for Read and Discuss Queries: In this version of a New York Times *article, we learn of the importance of an education in increasing the length and quality of our lives.*

Page 171
B Read and Discuss
To establish that an educated person seems to live longer: **How does the title tie into what you have read in the first two paragraphs?** Possible response: We hear a lot of ideas about living longer, but according to James Smith, staying in school is the most important factor in lengthening your life. **Follow-up: Is this all there is to it?** Possible response: Although education seems to be the major factor for a long life, not smoking and having supportive friends and family make a difference, too.

Page 172
A Vocabulary
Wealthy means "rich" or "well off."

C Reading Focus
Possible answers: underline: "She found information about a study from 1969 that showed a link between education and health."/ "In every country, forcing students to spend

more years in school meant that they lived longer lives."

Page 173
E Reading Focus
Students' opinions will vary, but explanations should include evidence from the text.

F Read and Discuss
To discern that while money does not necessarily ensure a long life, controlling risk factors does make a difference: **What did you learn from this article about lengthening your life?** Possible response: Managing risk factors like those that lead to heart disease and, in general, making healthy choices will extend lives. Being educated about risk factors is part of planning ahead and being in control of life.

Comprehension Wrap-Up
1. Possible response: Although I am young now, the decisions I make can have long-lasting consequences.

Page 174
Skills Practice
Use a Comparison Chart
Possible answers:
1. In many countries around the world, longer mandatory education results in longer life spans.
2. answer provided
3. Less informed people may begin smoking or make other unhealthy decisions.
4. Learning about good nutrition in school helps students avoid heart disease.

Page 175
Applying Your Skills
Informational Text Focus
Students' answers will vary considerably, but should contain persuasive techniques similar to those used in the article.

Reading Focus
Students' answers will vary, but should discuss the validity of the evidence they listed on the Skills Practice page to determine whether or not they find the author's conclusion convincing.

Vocabulary Review
1. education 2. isolated 3. expert

Holt Adapted Reader Answer Key

OPRAH TALKS ABOUT HER SOUTH AFRICAN "DREAMGIRLS"

Major Understanding for Read and Discuss Queries: *Students should understand that this informational piece is actually an interview between Diane Sawyer and Oprah Winfrey. They should recognize that Oprah's school provides a once in a lifetime opportunity for girls in South Africa, but students need to be aware of the opposition and criticism surrounding the school.*

Page 177
A Read and Discuss
To establish that the Oprah Winfrey Leadership Academy was opened for girls in South Africa: **What have you learned about the Oprah Winfrey Leadership Academy?** Possible response: It is a school that Oprah Winfrey opened for girls who live in South Africa. *To understand that many people believe that the school is a bit lavish for such a poor country:* **Follow-up: What do people think of the school?** Possible response: Although the school provides a wonderful opportunity for the girls, many feel that with its theater, library and African art everywhere, it is a bit excessive for such a poverty stricken country.

Page 178
B Vocabulary
An *opportunity* is a chance to accomplish something.

Page 179
C Read and Discuss
To discern that the girls are hard working and to recognize that many are attending the school in order to take care of their families: **What did you find out about the girls that are going to the academy?** Possible response: Many of them chose to attend the academy so that they could take care of their families. **Follow up: What does Oprah think about the girls?** Possible response: She wants them to be proud of themselves and not to be ashamed that they are poor. She is determined to do everything in her power to help them make it.

F Reading Focus
Possible answer: Oprah, out of the kindness of her heart, is providing these girls with a once-in-a-lifetime opportunity to attend a respectable school.

Comprehension Wrap-Up
1. Possible response: Due to her own underprivileged upbringing, Oprah feels she can relate to the South African girls. She believes, however, that money does not define a person.

Page 180
Skills Practice
Use a Citations and Assertions Chart
Possible answers:
Citation: Oprah kept her promise to South African leaders that she would pay to build a school for young girls.
Citation: Many of the girls attending Oprah's school come from poor homes with no electricity or running water.
Assertion: Oprah is a caring person, and she has done a marvelous thing by building this school and giving South African girls access to education.

Page 181
Applying Your Skills
Informational Text Focus
Quotations that students select will vary considerably.

Reading Focus
Students' answers may vary somewhat, but students should use the evidence provided to make an assertion about the Cougars baseball team—most likely that the Cougars will be the state championship again this year.

Vocabulary Review
1. opportunity 2. resistance

START THE DAY RIGHT!

Major Understanding for Read and Discuss Queries: *Students should understand that this is a brief television ad promoting healthy eating habits. They should recognize the importance and benefits of eating healthy foods. Also, students should comment on whether the ad was successful in getting its message across.*

Page 184
A Read and Discuss

To establish the scene: A classroom where most students are attentive, except for one boy who, apparently, didn't have breakfast or had a non-nutritional one: **What is going on in this classroom?** Possible response: Most of the students are engaged with the lesson, except for one boy. He seems to be sleepy and not paying attention. The ad makes it sound as if he's sleepy because he didn't have breakfast or his breakfast wasn't very nutritional. **Follow up: What point is the author trying to make?** Possible response: It's important to eat a good breakfast, or you'll end up like this sleepy boy!

C Language Coach
Circle: "(b) the strength to do active things without getting tired."

D Reading Focus
Possible answers: underline: "Studies show that the eating habits kids learn when they're young stay with them all of their lives. Unhealthy eating as children can lead to a variety of health problems in adulthood. These include everything from low energy and obesity to diabetes and heart disease."/ "Parents, you wouldn't let your kids go to school without their homework. Don't let them go without a good breakfast either."

Page 185
Applying Your Skills
Comprehension Wrap-Up
1. Possible response: This ad presented some good arguments about healthy eating. Students may want to take its advice into consideration.

Informational Text Focus
Possible answers:
1. Main message: Eating a healthy breakfast is important.
2. The message is a fact–something that can be proved true.
3. The intended audience is the parents of young children.
4. The author uses both logical and emotional appeals. Students' opinions may vary, but may indicate that the emotional appeals are more effective.
5. The author is trying to persuade the audience to set their kids on a healthy path for the rest of their lives.

Vocabulary Review

1. nutritious   **2.** irritable

SHINE-N-GROW: HAIR REPAIR THAT REALLY WORKS!

Major Understanding for Read and Discuss Queries: This advertisement presents students with information to examine and decide whether the ad is persuasive—is it too good to be true and why?

Page 187
B Read and Discuss
To establish what this advertisement is trying to sell: **What is the goal of this advertisement?** Possible response: This advertisement claims Shine-n-Grow can make your hair grow infinitely faster than it would if you didn't use the product. It also says it makes hair shinier—the ad wants you to buy the product.

D Vocabulary
According to the advertisement, these *nutrients* help hair grow.

Page 189
D Reading Focus
Yes. This is fallacious reasoning—more specifically, it's an example of the only-cause fallacy. This customer does not consider any other causes for his or her improved social life.

E Read and Discuss
To recognize that the "secret" hair ingredient and "happy customers" are ploys to entice buyers without solid research to say the product really works: **How do "secret" formulas and happy customers affect the way you think about this product?** Possible response: The secret formula of herbs makes us think this advertisement isn't truthful or is at least misleading because any good product should tell the consumer what's in it. However, reading the words of happy customers—though we don't know these customers really exist—makes me think, hey, maybe it does work.

Page 190
Skills Practice
Use a Reasoning Chart
Possible answers:

1. Hasty generalization: If you had your hair cut too short one time, you probably frequently wish that you could have longer hair.
2. Circular reasoning: Shine-n-Grow is the only shampoo that actually speeds up hair growth.
3. Only-cause fallacy: One customer claims to go on more dates since using Shine-n-Grow Shampoo.

Page 191
Applying Your Skills
Comprehension Wrap-Up
1. Possible response: This advertisement is not persuasive, as its reasoning seems faulty.

Informational Text Focus
1. Circular reasoning
2. Only-cause fallacy
3. Thoughtless generalization

Vocabulary Review
1. Draw a line to: "promise"
2. Draw a line to: "uncommon"
Students' sentences will vary, but should demonstrate an understanding of the selected vocabulary word.

BRAIN BREEZE

Major Understanding for Read and Discuss Queries: This advertisement presents students with information to examine and decide whether the ad is persuasive. Are you interested in buying this product? Why or why not?

Page 193
C Vocabulary
The *device* in question is the Brain Breeze—a gadget that supposedly improves brain functioning.

Page 194
A Vocabulary
Portable means "easily carried or transported."

B Reading Focus
Possible answer: underline: "Successful people understand how BRAIN BREEZE can help them."

Page 195
C Read and Discuss
To be able to analyze a set of contextual facts:
What have we learned about the Brain Breeze? Why does the author include Tony Fine's comment? Possible response: Brain Breeze is a product that claims it can act as a "mental power booster" by scientifically enhancing your concentration through the use of stimulating music and airflow. Tony Fine comments on how well the product worked for him, to show a "real life" example of how effective the product is.

E Reading Focus
Underline: "No more lost canes or forgetting to take prescription medicines!"

F Reading Focus
Students' answers may vary but should indicate that this is a bandwagon appeal. The advertisement is encouraging readers not to be the last person you know to act on the offer.

Page 196
Skills Practice
Use a Propaganda Chart
1. Name calling
2. Stereotype
3. Bandwagon appeal

Page 197
Applying Your Skills
Comprehension Wrap-Up
1. Possible response: All of the arguments put forth in this advertisement are just forms of propaganda. The ad is particularly shameless in that it uses the bandwagon appeal repeatedly.

Informational Reading Focus
Students' answers will vary considerably, but should illustrate students' understanding of each type of propaganda.

Vocabulary Review
Students' answers will vary. Possible answer: If you're constantly losing your *concentration* during class, try Brain Breeze—it will *enhance* your ability to focus.

SKILLS REVIEW

Page 198

Vocabulary Review

Students' answers will vary, considerably but should reflect an understanding of the vocabulary words selected for each question.

Page 199
Language Coach

Possible answers:
1. answer provided
2. complete: completely, completed, completes, completing.
3. nation: national, nationality, nations, nationalism.
4. enhance: enhancement, enhancer, enhanced, enhancing.

Oral Language Activity

Students' conversations will vary, but should reflect their knowledge of the types of persuasion they learned about in this Collection's readings.

Collection 7

THE SNEETCHES

Major Understanding for Read and Discuss Queries: Dr. Seuss's poem calls on readers to examine the poem more deeply than a small child might. Seuss illustrates the absurdity of creating social structures based on appearances. In addition, the poem reveals the way the greedy McBean takes advantage of the Sneetches' useless attempts to be better than others to fill his pockets with their money.

Page 203
B Read and Discuss

To set up that the Sneetches have segregated themselves according to having belly stars or not and that the Star-Belly Sneetches consider themselves a higher caliber Sneetch: **What has Dr. Seuss set up as the conflict between the Sneetches?** Possible response: Dr. Seuss presents two groups of Sneetches—with the Star-Belly Sneetches seeing themselves as superior to the Plain-Belly Sneetches. **Follow-up: What does the way the Star-Belly Sneetches treat the Plain-Belly Sneetches show us about them?** Possible response: The Star-Belly Sneetches might think they're

better than the Plain-Belly variety, but they are not nice creatures.

Page 204
C Reading Focus

Students should read lines 27–37 aloud.

Page 205
E Read and Discuss

To draw attention to the problem created for the first set of Star-Belly Sneetches now that everyone has a star: **How are the original Star-Belly Sneetches reacting to the news?** Possible response: They're determined to continue to set themselves apart to remain higher in status than the new Star-Belly Sneetches. **Follow-up: The original Star-Belly Sneetches say they are still the best Sneetches and the others are the worst, even though they all have stars now. What does this thinking show us about the situation?** Possible response: It seems that the original Star-Belly Sneetches only used the stars as an excuse to consider themselves better. They don't see the new Star-Belly Sneetches as equal even when the equalizing factor is now present in plain view.

F Vocabulary

Contraption means "machine" or "device."

Page 206
B Literary Focus

Line 69: A
Line 70: A
Line 71: B
Line 72: B

Page 207
C Read and Discuss

To establish that only through the insane events that followed the arrival of McBean and the subsequent loss of money do the Sneetches learn that the state of their bellies doesn't make one group better or worse than the other: **How does McBean influence the behavior of the Sneetches?** Possible response: McBean takes advantage of the Sneetches' perceived flaws to fill his pockets with their money. He is only too happy to help them solve their problem as they see it at a particular time. **Follow-up: How do the Sneetches react when McBean finally leaves?** Possible response: Instead of continuing to fight, they come to the conclusion that just having something on their

Holt Adapted Reader Answer Key

bellies or not doesn't make them better or worse.

Comprehension Wrap-Up
Possible responses:
1. This poem shows that what we look like does not matter; what matters more is who we are inside.
2. There are always people who like to take advantage of a situation and will try to make money anyway they can.

Page 208
Skills Practice
Use a Rhyme Scheme Chart
Lines 7–12:
Line 7: A
Line 8: A
Line 9: B
Line 10: B
Line 11: C
Line 12: C

Lines 85–92:
Line 85: A
Line 86: A
Line 87: B
Line 88: A
Line 89: C
Line 90: D
Line 91: E
Line 92: D

Page 209
Applying Your Skills
Literary Focus
Possible answers:
1. spaces   2. screams
3. pie   4. file

Students' lines of poetry will vary, but should correctly use end rhymes.

Reading Focus
Students' readings will vary depending on which lines they choose.
1. Answers should indicate the differences between reading poetry aloud and reading poetry silently.
2. Answers should indicate whether or not students found it fun to read the text out loud.

Vocabulary Review
1. synonyms   2. antonyms   3. synonyms

JOHN HENRY

Major Understanding for Read and Discuss Queries: Folk hero John Henry is a larger-than-life steel-worker. The students should notice the repetitive phrases throughout the poem that build the drama of the story.

Page 212
A Read and Discuss
To establish the character of John Henry and that he is taking on the captain's challenge: **What have you learned about John Henry so far?** Possible response: This John Henry is unusual! When he was a newborn, he picked up a hammer and talked about it being the death of him. Then later as an adult, we read about him having a job pounding steel with his hammer. **Follow up: What is the discussion between the captain and John Henry?** Possible response: The captain is bringing a steam drilling machine to do the job that John Henry has been doing with his hammer. Not to be outdone, John Henry says he'll beat the machine's output or die trying. **Follow up: How does this connect to what we first read about John Henry?** Possible response: When John Henry was a baby, he said, "the hammer's gonna be the death of me." So it seems that John Henry always knew of the struggle he would face.

B Literary Focus
Possible answer: This repetition helps readers imagine the sound of steel ringing over and over.

Page 213
D Reading Focus
Students' questions will vary, but should pertain to the content or style of the poem.

E Read and Discuss
To recognize John Henry's diligence in the face of his nemesis: **What has happened?** Possible response: John Henry beat the steam drill, pounding more steel than even the machine!

Page 214
A Read and Discuss
To understand that John Henry dies after his extreme efforts to beat the steam drill: **How do things turn out?** Possible response: John

Henry pushes himself too hard and dies, leaving behind his wife and son. **Follow up: What's the implication with the hammering that can still be heard?** Possible response: The distant sound of hammering makes it seem as if John Henry's memory lives on.

C Language Coach
Underline: "You could hold him in the palm of your hand"

D Literary Focus
Students' answers will vary, but may indicate that the final repetition serves as a continual reminder of John Henry.

Page 215
Applying Your Skills
Literary Focus
Possible answer:
John Henry was a man
I mean, he was a steel-driving man
Maybe he was just driving steel
But he was still John Henry, Lord, Lord!
He was still John Henry.

Reading Focus
Possible answers:
1. This poem is not meant to be realistic; these ideas just go to show how unique a man John Henry is.
2. This is exaggerated to show that John Henry is very strong.
3. This is also exaggerated to show both how big John Henry is and how young his son is.

Vocabulary Review
1. synonyms   2. antonyms   3. antonyms

ODE TO MI GATO

Major Understanding for Read and Discuss Queries: Students should appreciate the special bond shared by the speaker and his cat and should understand how each benefits from the relationship.

Page 217
C Read and Discuss
To establish that the speaker is describing his cat and what he likes: **What is the speaker telling you about his cat?** Possible response: He is talking about his white cat and all of the things he likes—the sun, milk, the rattle of the cat food, and the nuggets dropping into his bowl.

Page 219
B Vocabulary
Possible answer: *Rusty* means "covered with rust." It was easy to come up with this definition because *rusty* has the word *rust* within it.

C Literary Focus
Underline: "Like the rusty latch/ On a gate."

D Read and Discuss
To recognize the relationship the speaker has with his cat: **What have you learned about the relationship between the speaker and his cat?** Possible response: The speaker feels that his cat loves him for all of the things he did and still does for him—saved him from a dog, dresses him for Halloween, gives him milk, cheese and huevo/egg.

E Read and Discuss
To understand that although the speaker's cat may not be a great hunter, he appreciates the love he receives from his cat: **What point is the speaker making about his cat?** Possible response: Although his cat is not the greatest hunter, the speaker appreciates the love his cat gives him.

Page 220
A Literary Focus
Students' answers about picturing the cat will vary. Possible answers: "Like a clean sheet of paper."/ "Like a floating cloud."

Page 221
Applying Your Skills
Comprehension Wrap-Up
1. Possible response: Both the speaker and his cat love one another.

Literary Focus
Students' answers will vary, but should reflect an understanding of similes.

Reading Focus
Students' questions and answers will vary, but should address any questions that arose during reading of the text.

Vocabulary Review
1. abandoned   2. dangled

Page 222
Vocabulary Review

1. d.   6. a.
2. h.   7. j.
3. b.   8. f.
4. e.   9. g.
5. i.   10. c.

Students' sentences will vary, but should reflect an understanding of the vocabulary words.

Page 223
Language Coach
Students should put a check next to the first and third statements.

Writing Activity
Students' poems will vary, but should follow the presented pattern and reflect an understanding of similes.

Collection 8

BLANCA FLOR

Major Understanding for Read and Discuss Queries: In this fantastic tale, Juanito seeks his fortune in the world and teams up with Blanca Flor who has magical powers. By the end, they have the upper hand against the loathsome Don Ricardo who had been determined to ruin their happiness.

Page 228
A Language Coach
family

C Read and Discuss
Why do you think the author has Juanito talk to the audience here? Possible response: Juanito speaks directly to the audience to explain what a Duende is, as it's a mythical creature, and may be unfamiliar to the audience.

Page 229
D Literary Focus
Juanito and the Duende discuss where Juanito can find work.

E Reading Focus
Possible response: The stage directions help the reader picture a small opening in the trees for a narrow dirt path, which the Duende is pointing at.

Page 230
A Read and Discuss
To establish that Juanito, with his parents' blessing, has left to seek his fortune, and meets a forest Duende: **What do we know about Juanito and the Duende so far?** Possible response: Juanito, off to make his way in the world, meets the trick-playing Duende in the forest and the Duende sends Juanito down a path looking for a job.

Page 231
C Reading Focus
Students; answers may vary, but should indicate that Don Ricardo enters with a flourish, and is immediately a presence on stage.

D Literary Focus
Students' answers may vary, but should indicate that Juanito says these lines tentatively, since he has to "gather all his courage."

Page 232
B Read and Discuss
To introduce Blanca Flor and her captor, Don Ricardo: **What is going on with Juanito now?** Possible response: Juanito has met a girl named Blanca Flor, imprisoned by Don Ricardo, who offers Juanito an impossible job—by the next morning, Juanito is to move the water in the lake using only a thimble. Not only does the confident Juanito plan to accomplish the task, but he says he'll rescue Blanca Flor as well.

Page 234
A Vocabulary
Students' answers will vary but should indicate that a *barren* field is one with no crops, and is most likely empty.

B Vocabulary
"a sweeping movement"

Page 235

C Literary Focus

Circle: "shaking with fear"/ "very angry"

D Read and Discuss

To focus on the hapless Juanito, on Blanca Flor's magical powers, and on Don Ricardo's evil character: **How did Juanito's first two task turn out?** Possible response: When Juanito realizes he can't handle the job, Blanca Flor uses her powers to move the lake. Don Ricardo is furious that the task is completed and he demands another task be done—clear the land, plant, grow and harvest wheat for bread making the following day. Again, Blanca Flor's magic came to the rescue and furious Don Ricardo is planning a third task. Blanca Flor says they must leave quickly.

Page 236

A Literary Focus

This dialogue shows that Juanito and Blanca Flor are trying to escape from Don Ricardo. Blanca Flor says that she has used her powers to buy them some extra time to get away.

Page 237

B Read and Discuss

To appreciate the experiences in the story that are beyond reality (and can make for the fun in the adventures): **What is this part about?** Possible response: As Blanca Flor and Juanito prepare to leave, she spits three times into the fireplace and twice the spit answered Don Ricardo's calls. By then, Don Ricardo senses what the pair is up to and chases Juanito and Blanca Flor. **Follow-up: Why does Blanca Flor spit in the fire?** Possible response: Blanca Flor spit into the fire so that after they left, the spit would answer Don Ricardo and they'd have a head start running away from him. There is so much fantasy in this story that it mixes in fun with the evil done by the villain Don Ricardo.

Page 238

B Read and Discuss

To reinforce that Blanca Flor's powers are keeping the pair one step ahead of Don Ricardo: **What did you find out, and what does this say about Blanca Flor?** Possible response: In order to fool Don Ricardo, Blanca Flor turns Juanito into an old man who rings a

bell while changing herself into a statue near the church. Blanca Flor sounds like someone to have around when there's trouble!

Page 239

C Literary Focus

Possible answer: Juanito and Blanca Flor are tired, but they know that they are not safe yet and must keep running.

Page 240

A Literary Focus

Students should read the dialogue aloud, taking the stage directions into consideration.

Page 242

A Read and Discuss

To draw attention to Blanca Flor's next clever trick and Don Ricardo's reaction:
How is the escape going now? Possible response: Blanca Flor again changes the pair into a scarecrow and a stalk of corn by tossing her magical comb. When Don Ricardo becomes suspicious, Blanca Flor slyly transforms the pair into ducks that fly away from him. **Follow-up: How does Don Ricardo respond?** Possible response: So that the two will not be together, Don Ricardo puts a curse on Juanito and Blanca Flor, saying "the first person to embrace him will cause him to forget you forever."

Page 243

B Reading Focus

Possible answer: Don Ricardo's lands are in a forest, near a river. Juanito's family lives in a village, where there are more people and buildings.

Page 244

A Literary Focus

Possible answer: Juanito's parents miss their son, are worried about him, and want to see him soon.

Page 245

C Read and Discuss

To emphasize that Don Ricardo's curse is working: **What does this conversation show us about Don Ricardo's curse?** Possible response: Juanito was going to explain about Blanca Flor to his parents when he reached his home. However, when his parents hugged

Holt Adapted Reader Answer Key

him, he couldn't seem to remember anything about being away and certainly nothing about Blanca Flor. His parents think he should meet a neighbor girl who'd make a good wife. Poor Blanca Flor—Don Ricardo's curse is working and keeping the pair apart.

Page 246
A Reading Focus
Possible answer: The stage directions explain that the doves are actually actors in costumes.

Page 247
B Language Coach
In English, *Blanca Flor* means "white flower."

C Read and Discuss
To understand how Blanca Flor breaks Don Ricardo's spell: **How does Blanca Flor's plan break Don Ricardo's spell?** Possible response: Because Blanca Flor is heartbroken that Juanito can't remember her because of Don Ricardo's curse, she plans to win Juanito back by breaking the spell with a gift of doves that sing words to remind Juanito of Blanca Flor. Once Don Ricardo's curse has been broken, the pair can be together.

Page 248
Comprehension Wrap-Up
Possible responses:
1. Blanca Flor's magic is stronger. She is able to perform the impossible tasks Don Ricardo sets for Juanito. She can fool Don Ricardo with her spit, and by transforming herself and Juanito. She is able to escape by turning herself and Juanito into ducks, and in the end she even breaks Don Ricardo's final curse.
2. The story has many parts that are common in fairy tales. The hero is on an adventure and meets magical people and creatures. He must perform three impossible tasks. He and his love must escape from an evil magician and transform three times. The

woman must win her love back after magic has made him forget her.
3. Blanca Flor did not realize she had so much power until she tried to use it to help Juanito.

Page 249
Applying Your Skills
Literary Focus
Students' answers will vary, but students should select fairy tale scenes to which they can apply dialogue and stage directions.

Reading Focus
Students' drawings will vary, but should reflect details from the play.

Vocabulary Review
1. barren
2. apprehensively
3. valiant
4. flourish

SKILLS REVIEW

Page 250
Vocabulary Review
1. Yes
2. No
3. Yes
4. Yes
5. No

Students' sentences will vary, but should reflect an understanding of the words *valiant* and *display*.

Page 251
Language Coach
maestro: master
familia: family
capitán: captain
blanca: white
flor: flower

Oral Language Activity
Students' performances should incorporate both the play's dialogue and stage directions.

Holt Adapted Reader Answer Key

First Course

Collection 1

AMIGO BROTHERS

Major Understanding for Read and Discuss Queries: "Amigo Brothers" explores the complicated world of Antonio and Felix, who are best friends and boxing competitors. Antonio and Felix demonstrate that honor in boxing and honor in friendship can be achieved simultaneously.

Page 3
C Read and Discuss
To elicit that the Golden Gloves tournament is more than just a boxing event—it is a way for disadvantaged boys to get into a big-time sport: **What is the author telling us about the Golden Gloves tournament?** Possible response: The tournament allows young boxers to dream about making their lives better and provides a concrete step in that direction.

Page 4
B Read and Discuss
To further establish the boys' dedication to boxing: **How does the boys' decision to train separately add to what we know about Antonio and Felix?** Possible response: It further demonstrates how much they care about boxing and for each other—each boy wants to give the other and himself the best opportunity to win.

C Vocabulary
Here, *trunks* means "very short trousers."

Page 5
D Literary Focus
Underline: "Felix knew then that Antonio wasn't pulling any punches. Both would fight to win."

F Read and Discuss
To further establish that each boy must find a way around the other's strengths in order to win: **What can we learn from the conversation between the boys and their**

trainers? Possible response: Each trainer is encouraging his boxer to use his strengths against the other's weakness.

Page 6
A Reading Focus
The crowd is roaring at first, but then they go silent.

B Read and Discuss
To establish that the boys demolished each other in the ring, but their friendship is still the most important thing to them: **What is going on now?** Possible response: The boys left the ring arm-in-arm before the winner was announced. **Follow-up: How does this connect to what we know about the boys?** Possible response: They are honorable in the way they fought and in the way they treat their friendship.

C Literary Focus
Possible answer: Both boys fought well, and they left as equals.

Comprehension Wrap-Up
1. Possible response: They take fighting seriously but they take their friendship seriously as well, and are honorable in both.

Page 7
Applying Your Skills
Literary Focus
1. b   2. d
3. c   4. a

Reading Focus
1. comparison   2. contrast
3. contrast   4. comparison

Vocabulary Review
1. abdomen   2. trunks

EMPRESS THEODORA

Major Understanding for Read and Discuss Queries: This article demonstrates the way extraordinary people can come from any economic or social group. Empress Theodora's story is even more impressive in that it occurred in ancient times when it was very rare for a woman to move from one social stratum to another or wield significant power.

Page 9
A Read and Discuss
To set up that Theodora led an extraordinary life (even though a traveling actor was viewed as low class back in 500 A.D.) that only gets more fascinating when she meets the man of her dreams—a man she isn't permitted to marry: **What does the author set up for us about Theodora's life?** Possible response: The author tells us Empress Theodora grew up poor; even though she eventually became the Empress.

Page 10
A Reading Focus
Possible answers:
Main idea: Laws to better protect women and children.
1. Supporting detail: Gave divorced women rights, like the ability to care for their children.
2. Supporting detail: Women could now own property.
3. Supporting detail: Parents could no longer leave infant girls to die.

B Read and Discuss
To firmly establish Theodora's strength and its influence on history: **How do Theodora's actions during the riot add to what we know about her?** Possible response: Her willingness to trade her life for their empire and ability to inspire the men to continue fighting resulted in them saving Constantinople and securing their legacy. This is another example of her uncommon wisdom and gumption—especially in light of her original commoner status.

C Vocabulary
Students' answers will vary, but should indicate that Theodora and Justinian *improve* the quality of the drinking water by adding new pipes and building shelters for the homeless.

Comprehension Wrap-Up
1. Possible response: She might have told them to defend their home and to have honor and courage in times of difficulty.

Page 11
Applying Your Skills
Informational Text Focus

1. B   2. C

Possible answers:
Main idea: Theodora is born poor…
Detail 1: Theodora started as an ordinary actor.
Detail 2: Later in life, Theodora helped save Constantinople with a great speech.
Main idea: Theodora uses her position…
Detail 1: Divorced women gained rights.
Detail 2: Women could now own property.

Vocabulary Review
1. convinced   2. improve   3. speech

THE HIPPODROME

Major Understanding for Read and Discuss Queries: *This piece details the way the Great Constantinople Hippodrome served its citizens and details its demise at the hands of invaders.*

Page 13
A Read and Discuss
To recognize the Hippodrome served as the center of Constantinople life and that it seems to be a sophisticated arena for that time in history: **What is the author telling you about the Hippodrome?** Possible response: The Hippodrome seemed to provide a center for all aspects of city life.

Page 14
A Vocabulary
"riot" and "revolt"

B Reading Focus
Possible answer: Supporters of two teams join together to protest against Justinian, but their riot is violently put down.

C Read and Discuss
To establish the demise of the Hippodrome after the city was overtaken and renamed Istanbul: **How does the Hippodrome from the Byzantine Empire compare to the Hippodrome that exists today?** Possible response: It's far from grand today. After Constantinople was attacked and named Istanbul, the Turks used the stones from the great stadium to build new buildings. Now, the remnants of the great space are few and far between.

Holt Adapted Reader Answer Key

Comprehension Wrap-Up

Possible responses:

1. They took the Hippodrome apart. Maybe with their new power over the city, they wanted to start something new instead of keeping something that the rulers before them started.
2. Some students might wish that the Hippodrome was maintained as a piece of history, while others might agree with the decision the Turks made.

Page 15
Applying Your Skills
Informational Text Focus

1. A   2. B

Possible answers:

First box: The Hippodrome was a popular and important stadium.

Second Box: There was a big protest in the Hippodrome called the Nika revolt.

Third Box: Ottoman Turks took over the city and ruined the Hippodrome.

Students' summaries will vary, but should include the three main events they listed in the preceding exercise.

Vocabulary Review

1. stadium   2. ceremonies
3. protest   4. ruins

SKILLS REVIEW

Page 16
Vocabulary Review

1. b.   2. c.
3. a.   4. d.

Students' sentences will vary, but should reflect an understanding of the vocabulary definitions.

Page 17
Language Coach

1. Circle "able." It changes the meaning to "giving comfort."
2. Circle "ly." It changes the meaning to "like a friend."
3. Circle "ness." It changes the meaning to "Being eager."
4. Circle "ity" It changes the meaning to "the state of being similar."

Writing Activity

Students' summaries will vary. Students should begin with a statement of the main ideas and should include the title of the selection and at least two supporting details.

Collection 2

RIKKI-TIKKI-TAVI

Major Understanding for Read and Discuss Queries: In this magical tale of friendship, a mongoose and a family depend on each other for survival. As their relationship develops, we are invited into Rikki-tikki-tavi's world where we learn about nature and an animal's instinct to survive.

Page 21
A Read and Discuss

To establish the character of Rikki-tikki-tavi: **What has the author told you about Rikki-tikki-tavi so far?** Possible response: He is a mongoose who is going to fight some sort of war.

Page 22
A Read and Discuss

To connect with the previous idea of the conflict between Rikki-tikki-tavi and Nag: **What just happened between Rikki-tikki and Nag and his wife?** Possible response: Nag and his wife, Nagaina got into a fight with Rikki-tikki-tavi, and Rikki-tikki-tavi bit Nag's wife, leaving her badly injured. **Follow-up: How does this connect with what we just talked about?** Possible response: Nag and his wife knew that Rikki-tikki-tavi would eventually try to kill them, so they were ready for a fight.

B Reading Focus

Possible answer: Rikki-tikki bites Nag's wife, Nagaina, and then kills the other snake, Karait.

C Vocabulary

Possible answer: Rikki-tikki did not see why Chuchundra would be afraid of him or assume he would kill him.

Holt Adapted Reader Answer Key

D Literary Focus

Rikki-tikki's fight with Karait is a conflict because it is a struggle that makes the story more interesting.

Page 23
E Read and Discuss

To draw attention to Nag and Nagaina's plan to kill the family, so that Rikki-tikki-tavi will leave the house and then they can have the garden to themselves: **What are Nag and Nagaina up to?** Possible response: They are planning to kill the family, so that Rikki-tikki-tavi will leave. Then, they will have the garden to themselves again.

Page 24
A Read and Discuss

What is Rikki-tikki up to? Possible response: Rikki-tikki is trying to come up with a plan to kill Nagaina.

C Read and Discuss

To understand that Nagaina has come to get revenge on the family that she thought killed Nag, but that Rikki-tikki-tavi interrupts her plan by challenging her to a fight: **What is Nagaina up to?** Possible response: She has come to kill Teddy and the family because she thought they killed Nag.

Page 25
D Literary Focus

Underline: "'The cobras are all dead. And if any more come, I'm here,'"/ "From then on, he protected the yard. No cobra ever again dared to enter it."

Comprehension Wrap Up

1. Possible response: The mother goes from being unsure about keeping Rikki-tikki to being happy he was there to save their lives. Teddy and his father become happier with Rikki-tikki each time he protects them.

Page 26
Skills Practice
Use a Concept Map

Possible answers:
1. Fighting Nagaina in the yard.
2. Fighting Karait.
3. Fighting Nag in the bathroom.
4. Fighting and killing Nagaina down the rabbit hole.

Page 27
Applying Your Skills
Literary Focus

1. nature   2. himself   3. villain

Reading Focus

Possible answers:
1. Rikki-tikki stands in his way.
2. He plans to kill Teddy's family so that Rikki-tikki will go away and the garden will be theirs to hatch their eggs.

Vocabulary Review

1. slither   2. scornfully

FLEA PATROL

Major Understanding for Read and Discuss Queries: "Flea Patrol" reveals the surprising existence of the plague in the world today. However, the article also illustrates the plague's weakened influence in causing great death as it did centuries before.

Page 29
A Read and Discuss

To set up that cases of the plague have been uncovered in national forests, in dead animals: **What has the author set up for us?** Possible response: The author has told us that the plague was recently uncovered at national parks. **Follow-up: Why might park rangers worry about this news getting out to the public?** Possible response: When people hear the plague is alive and well, they panic even though there've been no reported cases of people catching it from the fleas who carry it. The rangers don't want people to stay away from the park because of unfounded fear.

Page 30
A Vocabulary

Antibiotics treat disease.

B Reading Focus

at the bottom of the pyramid

C Read and Discuss

To establish that although there are numerous isolated accounts of the plague in rodents and even some humans, there is little risk of getting it or dying from it: **The author gives you a lot of examples here. What is the author telling you about bubonic plague?** Possible response: The examples show us that even though the plague still exists, humans are for the most part safe from getting it and normally won't die from it.

Page 31
Applying Your Skills
Comprehension Wrap-Up
1. Possible response: The Black Death killed millions of people during the Middle Ages, but there are very few cases of it today because we can control it and treat it better now.

Informational Text Focus
1. C   2. B

Possible answers:
1. Main idea: Park rangers are fighting the spread of plague in some national parks.
2. Important detail: Plague is spread by rodents and fleas.
3. Less important detail: In 2006, a woman in Los Angeles was treated for plague.

Vocabulary Review
Students' answers will vary, but should relate to the article and incorporate all three vocabulary words.

THE BLACK DEATH

Major Understanding for Read and Discuss Queries: This article illustrates the impact the Plague had on an enormous number of people. The article also details the way people inadvertently spread the disease while trying to escape it.

Page 33
B Reading Focus
You can learn about which California standards are met by this chapter, and you can also find out that there is a video to watch.

Page 34
B Read and Discuss
To establish the breadth and depth of the Black Death: **How did the world deal with the Black Death?** Possible response: The plague, which consisted of several powerful strains, was impossible to contain. People dealt with the plague by burying the dead, dying themselves, or fleeing their villages.
Follow-up: What happened when villagers

left? Possible response: The villagers, who fled when people in their town started dropping dead, probably spread it to other villages, expanding the crisis.

C Reading Focus
Possible answer: The Reading Check questions only deal with this page about the Black Death; the Section 4 Assessment questions deal with everything in Section 4.

Page 35
D Read and Discuss
To discern that the graphic clearly illustrates the easy transport and transfer of the plague: **What does the graphic help you understand?** Possible response: The graphic shows us how quickly and easily the plague was passed. The graphic creates an image for us that sticks in our minds and makes it easy to picture how the plague spread so easily.

Page 36
A Reading Focus
Possible answers:
1. Ships from Asia brought goods for trade as well as the fleas that spread the plague.
2. Garbage and dirty conditions helped the plague spread quickly within Europe.

Page 37
Applying Your Skills
Comprehension Wrap-Up
1. Possible response: No, it could not spread the same way in our society today. Living conditions are much cleaner, medicine is much better, and information about how to stop the spread of a plague can be passed on to more people in a shorter amount of time.

Informational Text Focus
1. c.   2. b.

Students' answers will vary, but should include the full heading, a clear statement of the main idea expressed in that section, and a brief explanation of how that section illustrates the main idea.

Vocabulary Review
Students' answers will vary, but should correctly use both vocabulary words in a complete sentence.

ON PREVENTING PLAGUE

Major Understanding for Read and Discuss Queries: This graphic communicates a dire feel—indicating sickness or death. Even though the words are in a different language, seeing the graphic would make us hesitate before venturing further into a particular space.

Page 40
A Read and Discuss
To establish the strength of illustrations in communicating a warning: **What does this graphic let us know?** Possible response: In the context of the time a person would have seen this illustration and been warned that something dire was nearby. A person familiar with the plague would understand the illustration's meaning.

B Vocabulary
Prohibited means "not allowed."

C Reading Focus
Students' answers may include any three of the following:
1. The dead must be buried before sunrise or after sunset.
2. The constables must know about the burial.
3. No neighbors or friends can take the body to the church.
4. No children are allowed near the body or grave.
5. All graves will be at least six feet deep.

Page 41
Applying Your Skills
Comprehension Wrap-Up
1. Possible response: Students should discuss the impact of pictures in explaining things (how "a picture is worth a thousand words") and should address the particular illustration in question in relation to this concept. Responses should also explain how, as conditions and times change, illustrations' meanings can change. For example, an illustration might no longer represent a current danger, but may now represent a piece of history.

Informational Text Focus
Students' answers will vary, but may include: Watchmen: People who guard buildings at night.
Isolation: The state of being alone or apart.

Corpse: Dead body.
1. Possible answer: A glossary can teach you the definitions of some of the important words in the manual.
2. Students' answers will vary, but should demonstrate an understanding of the difference between a glossary and an index. For example, an index will have more entries than a glossary but will not include definitions of terms.

Vocabulary Review
1. infectious **2.** physician **3.** fit

SIGNS

Major Understanding for Read and Discuss Queries: This short piece illustrates the ease with which a sign can communicate an idea.

Page 43
A Read and Discuss
To establish the ease with which simple graphics communicate information: **What do signs tell us? What do these signs tell us?** Possible Response: Some signs warn us about dangerous things. Other signs tell us where certain people or animals have special access—like the dog park sign.

C Reading Focus
Possible answers: The red line means "no." Another sign like this might be a "no left turn" sign.

Page 44
B Vocabulary
Possible answer: It means that the symbol used to show a biohazard did not have any specific meaning before the sign was created.

Page 45
Applying Your Skills
Comprehension Wrap-Up
Possible responses:
1. The signs are easy to understand because their pictures and colors are easy to figure out. Also, most of us have grown up seeing them our entire lives.
2. Some modern signs would not make sense to me if I were living in 1900. For instance, methods of transportation have changed since 1900. Signs reflect the time periods and cultures in which they are created.

Holt Adapted Reader Answer Key

Informational Text Focus

  1. a.   **2.** d.

Students' signs will vary. The signs drawn should be written and colored in accurately, based on whichever sign the student chooses, followed by a written explanation of what the sign means.

Vocabulary Review

  1. biohazard   **2.** pharmacy   **3.** distinct

SKILLS REVIEW

Page 46
Vocabulary Review

1. rodent	**2.** slither	**3.** plague
4. accurate	**5.** infected	**6.** peasants
7. physician	**8.** pharmacy	

Students' sentences will vary, but should reflect an understanding of the vocabulary words.

Page 47
Language Coach

1. guard	**2.** scorn	**3.** ill
4. infect	**5.** instruct	

Oral Language Activity
Possible answers:
  1. A newspaper article tells you facts about current events.
  2. An instruction manual explains how to do a task.
  3. It usually has a table of contents, glossary, and index.
  4. The most important information goes first, then important details, and then less-important details.

Collection 3

THE WAR OF THE WALL

Major Understanding for Read and Discuss Queries: The people of Taliaferro Street are given a beautiful gift from an unlikely person. The community learns appearances can be deceiving and first impressions aren't always accurate.

Page 51
A Read and Discuss
To begin to establish the great emotion attached to the wall and how the painter lady causes problems: **What is the author letting you know about this wall?** Possible response: The wall is a touchstone of sorts for the community—the list of ways it's used is long and demonstrates that the wall means more than simply brick and mortar to the people who live there. It seems that a stranger—a woman—is painting it. **Follow-up: What might the narrator mean when he says Jimmy Lyons was never coming home from the war in Vietnam?** Possible response: He must have died in the war.

D Read and Discuss
To recognize that Lou is impressed with the painter's work, but the narrator doesn't let a little art appreciation interfere with his disgruntlement: **What does it mean that Lou and the narrator were at war?** Possible response: The narrator is so angry about what the painter is doing that he won't let anyone even admit that her work is impressive.

Page 52

B Read and Discuss
To further delineate the painter's distant personality and the narrator's refusal to find anything positive about her: **What is happening between the community members and the painter?** Possible response: Some of the people are making an effort to talk to and welcome the painter but she hardly even looks at them or talks to them. **Follow-up: How does this add to our picture of the painter?** Possible response: We can't say for sure. Her actions make her seem even colder, but maybe she is just concentrating, as Lou suggested.

D Literary Focus
Possible answer: They want to cover the wall in spray paint because they are angry that the painter lady is painting it.

E Read and Discuss
To discern that there is a big crowd excitedly milling around the wall: **What is happening at the wall?** Possible response: Something exciting must be happening.

Page 53
F Vocabulary
Students' answers will vary, but should indicate the flowers as a clue.

G Reading Focus
Possible answer: It now appears that the painter lady was doing something positive for the neighborhood, rather than something negative and intrusive.

I Read and Discuss
To establish that the painter had a larger stake in the wall than the community ever imagined: **How does this writing in the wall add to what we know about the painter lady?** Possible response: The wall meant a lot to her—although maybe not as much as it did to the people who lived there—and she understood the essence of the town and the people in it, and was connected to it herself through her cousin, Jimmy Lyons.

Comprehension Wrap-Up
Possible responses:
1. The narrator did not understand or care to understand the reason why the painter lady wanted to paint the wall. He should have been more accepting so that he could learn about and embrace other people's differences.
2. The painter was concentrating on getting a message across in her painting. She incorporated Lou and the narrator into the wall, showing them in situations in which they are learning and opening up to new things.

Page 54
Skills Practice
Use a Cause and Effect Map
Possible answers:
1. The painter lady was painting the wall that he loved.
2. She wanted to complete her painting; to do so, she needed to concentrate.

Page 55
Applying Your Skills
Literary Focus
1. Possible answer: The narrator and Lou wanted her to leave because she was painting the wall and they liked the wall the way it was before.
2. Possible answer: She wanted to paint something nice for the neighborhood that

was also a memorial to her cousin, who had died in the war.

Reading Focus
Possible answer: The painter lady may have told him what it was she was painting and the narrator would not have felt animosity towards her.

Vocabulary Review
1. vine   2. dedicate   3. allowance

BORDERS OF BASEBALL: U.S. AND CUBAN PLAY

Major Understanding for Read and Discuss Queries: This piece presents two views of baseball. One depicts a more commercialized version where fans idolize individual players who do their best to further their own careers, just to make as much money as possible. The other version of baseball occurs in more humble stadiums where teams are admired and players play for the pride and traditions associated with baseball in Cuba.

Page 57
A Read and Discuss
To recognize that the author's focus will have the students think about a deeper level of baseball—the traditions—not just the surface rules: **What is the author setting up for you in the first paragraph?** Possible response: The author wants us to pay attention to the traditions of baseball in both countries, not just the rules which are similar in both the USA and Cuba.

Page 58
B Vocabulary
In this case, *professional* means "earning a living by being an expert at something."

C Reading Focus
Possible answers: In the U.S., fans are usually separated from the players by a fence. In Cuba, they are not; In Cuba, fans do not ask players for autographs. In the U.S., this is a common practice among fans; In U.S. ballparks, team logos are everywhere; Ticket prices are higher in the U.S. than in Cuba.

D Read and Discuss
To consider the influence of each country's culture on the way the game is presented to

fans—America's stadiums and its baseball experience is rooted in commerce while the low-key Cuban stadium experience is rooted in unity and pride: **What is the connection between culture and each country's presentation of baseball?** Possible response: In America, fans often rush to obtain autographs from individual players. In Cuba, the stadiums are more plain and the game seems to be the focus, instead of merchandise and individual players. Fans seem to view the teams as a whole and the game as a source of pride for everyone—even the fans.

Page 59
Applying Your Skills
Comprehension Wrap-Up
Possible responses:
1. We might enjoy not having the fences in the ballpark so we could have better access for interacting and getting autographs from players, but we would have to get used to all of the other differences.
2. Baseball in Cuba is played for the nation, indicating national pride.

Informational Text Focus
   1. B

Possible answers:
Baseball in the U.S.: Players work for privately owned teams, tickets are $14–$15, and stadiums have fences to separate fans and players.
Baseball in Cuba: Players are state workers, ticket prices are pennies, and stadiums do not have fences.
Similarities: The game rules are the same in both places.

Vocabulary Review
   1. professionals
   2. compete

SKILLS REVIEW

Page 60
Vocabulary Review
   1. to reply
   2. gifted
   3. paid for a job
   4. in honor of

Students' sentences will vary, but should correctly use both vocabulary words.

Page 61
Language Coach
   1. What is happening?
   2. Smell the exhaust from that truck!
   3. What do you think about that?
   4. Let me see!

Writing Activity
Students' answers will vary, but should include reasons to support their opinion of whether or not the article presents a balanced view.

Collection 4

AFTER TWENTY YEARS

Major Understanding for Read and Discuss Queries: After Twenty Years provides a surprising twist that demonstrates why choosing a quiet, "plodding" life might not be such a bad thing.

Page 65
A Read and Discuss
To establish the peaceful setting and the striking, confident nature of the policeman: **What picture is the author painting for us?** Possible response: The author is showing us the sleepy beat that an established though not showy policeman is patrolling.

Page 66
A Read and Discuss
To elicit that the man in the doorway is waiting for a friend whom he promised to meet twenty years after and that he must care a lot about the person to make the long trip: **What is happening with the man in the doorway?** Possible response: The man is waiting for the friend he had dinner with twenty years before at the very same place. **Follow-up: How do you know that he thinks highly of his old friend?** Possible response: He has good memories of him and thinks highly of his character.

Holt Adapted Reader Answer Key

C Vocabulary

Students' sentences will vary, but should use the word *sharp* in the correct context.

Page 67
D Reading Focus

Possible answer: This observation hints that this man may not be Jimmy.

F Read and Discuss

How are things going for the two old friends? Possible response: Not good. Bob has just noticed that the man he is walking arm-in-arm with is not who he thought he was.

G Read and Discuss

To discern that Jimmy had shown up to meet Bob on time—he was the patrolman—and that Jimmy must still have a soft-spot for Bob: **What does it show us about Jimmy that he did not arrest Bob when he first recognized him?** Possible response: Jimmy must still have good memories of Bob and even though his values force him to make sure his friend pays for his crimes, Jimmy can't bring himself to embarrass Bob himself.

H Literary Focus

Possible answer: He knew all along that the policeman in the beginning of the story was Jimmy Wells.

Comprehension Wrap Up

1. Possible response: Bob cannot believe that his old friend Jimmy is the policeman who ordered his arrest.

Page 68
Skills Practice
Use a Predictions Chart

Possible answers:
1. The policeman is walking down the street late at night in the rain when all the stores are closed.
2. The policeman happens to be walking down this particular street at this odd time at night in this terrible weather because he is on his way to meet Bob—which tells us that he is Jimmy.
3. Bob notices that Jimmy looks taller.
4. This is to hint that it is really not Jimmy at all, but instead, another man—a man who has been sent to arrest Bob.

Page 69
Applying Your Skills

Literary Focus

Possible answers:
First box: Bob must know that Jimmy is a policeman, because policemen may encounter a life-threatening risk on the job.
Second box: That is a very vague statement. "I work for the city" could mean that you work as a street sweeper or a garbage collector, or it could mean that you are a policeman who works to keep the city safe.

Reading Focus

Students' answers will vary, but students should be sure to include their original predictions of how the story would end and whether or not the actual ending surprised them. Students should be able to explain their answers.

Vocabulary Review
  1. sharp   2. fortune

USER FRIENDLY

Major Understanding for Read and Discuss Queries: A young boy who is the school "nerd" is befriended by his computer. At first, he is thrilled with his computer's ability to become his friend, but then realizes their friendship might be more than he bargained for. The story has an ironic ending and adds a nice element of surprise for the reader.

Page 71
A Read and Discuss

To establish the main character, Kevin, and his computer, Louis: **What has the author told you so far about Kevin and Louis?** Possible response: There is a boy named Kevin who is getting ready for school, and apparently, his computer, Louis, serves to help him keep track of his life.

Page 72
A Vocabulary

Personality means "the qualities that form an individual's character."

C Read and Discuss

To draw attention to what the kids at school think of Kevin and to understand why Louis is a "special" computer: **What new information has the author given us about Kevin?** Possible response: He doesn't have any friends and the kids at school avoid him.

         Holt Adapted Reader Answer Key

Follow-up: What new information has the author given us about Louis? Louis isn't your typical "store" computer. Kevin's dad built and programmed it himself.

Page 73
E Vocabulary
Possible answer: Adding -*y* makes the word an adjective, so *nerdy* means "like a nerd."

F Literary Focus
Possible Answer: Kevin has feelings for Ginny, which relates to the themes of love and friendship. Kevin is finally brave enough to talk to Ginny, and she humiliates him. This emphasizes how he feels unpopular and relates to the theme of loneliness.

G Literary Focus
Possible Answer: Kevin is looking for friendship, and since the computer wants to help Kevin, it is acting like a friend to him.

Page 75
C Read and Discuss
To understand the role the modem plays in Louis's newfound skills: **What is the importance of the modem?** Possible response: Kevin's father had put the latest modem model into Louis, which explains how Louis was able to acquire so much information in such a short amount of time. **Follow-up: What does Kevin think about the "conversation" he had with Louis?** Possible response: Although the modem was able to access information like a normal computer, the modem was not responsible for Louis' ability to talk to Kevin and his ability to give him "unprogrammed" responses—so Kevin is still baffled.

D Literary Focus
Possible answer: These problems relate to the theme of bullying and, possibly, getting revenge or standing up for one's self later in the story.

Page 76
A Read and Discuss
To draw attention to Kevin's suspicion of Louis: **Now what is going on between Kevin and Louis?** Possible response: Kevin suspects that Louis is responsible for making the phone calls to Ginny. **Follow-up: What seems to be the new problem?** Possible response: Kevin told Louis that Chuck came after him and

Louis signed off abruptly. Kevin is afraid now that Louis will try to go after Chuck.

Page 77
C Read and Discuss
To reinforce the idea that Louis has struck again: **What has the author told us is going on with the Linke family?** Possible response: Chuck, who had threatened Kevin, has been arrested for sending a call threatening the president's life, and the rest of the family is receiving truckloads of junk mail. **Follow-up: What does this situation have to do with Kevin and Louis?** Possible response: More than likely, Louis is seeking revenge for the things they did to Kevin, and Kevin suspects as much.

D Read and Discuss
To establish that Kevin has decided he must put an end to Louis' actions: **What does Kevin think about Louis's actions?** Possible response: Kevin realizes that Louis has become dangerous and he must put a stop to his actions by pulling the plug. **Follow-up: If Kevin realizes he must stop Louis, why does he say he feels "so bad about doing it?"** Possible response: Kevin feels bad because Louis was his only friend and he was only hurting people who had hurt Kevin.

Page 78
A Read and Discuss
To appreciate the ironic ending and how Kevin feels about Louise: **What did we just find out about Louis?** Kevin's father printed out data that had been stored in memory. Ironically, Louis's name was actually 'Louise' and 'she' was in love with Kevin.

Page 79
B Literary Focus
Possible answers: Kevin did not realize that Louise was in love with him. Now Kevin is sad about the loss of the only friend he ever had who actually loved him, which relates to the themes of love, friendship, and loneliness in the story.

Comprehension Wrap-Up
Possible responses:
1. Kevin was always lonely and found out too late that his computer was the one friend who ever loved him. Now Kevin's loneliness is worse than ever before.

2. "User friendly" is a term which refers to computers that are easy for people to use. In this story, the term also means that the computer was actually "friendly" to its user.

Page 80
Skills Practice
Use a Concept Map
Possible answers:
1. Kevin doesn't have any friends at school.
2. Kevin has a crush on Ginny, but she does not feel the same way about him.
3. Chuck, Ginny's brother, bullies Kevin and other kids "stay away" from Kevin at school.
4. Kevin's dad gives him a computer with a built-in personality program, so that Kevin would feel like he had a friend. But his father's plan did not work right, and now, Kevin is even lonelier than before.

Page 81
Applying Your Skills
Literary Focus
Students' answers will vary, but should summarize the story's plot and identify the main theme.

Reading Focus
Students' answers will vary, but students should make comparisons between "User Friendly" and another story, movie or poem that has a similar plot, topic or theme.

Vocabulary Review
1. instantly   2. demanded   3. personality

ANNABEL LEE

Page 82
Preparing to Read
Reading Focus
Possible answers:
1. Summary: A man mourns over his departed love, recalling the powerful love they shared and will forever share – a love which he believes caused the angels to be jealous and take her away.
2. Theme: Lost love; tragedy.

Major Understanding for Read and Discuss Queries: This powerful poem represents Poe's anguish over the loss of his very young wife and provides a possible explanation for why she was taken from him so soon.

Page 83
A Read and Discuss
To establish the two main characters, the love they shared, and the angels' jealousy of that love: **What is the author setting up for you?** Possible response: The narrator is talking about the love he shared with a woman. He describes their love as being very powerful. **Follow up: What did the angels think of this love?** Possible response: They were jealous of this love.

B Literary Focus
Possible answer: Although the speaker and Annabel Lee are young, their love is strong. Their age relates to the theme of powerful love. The narrator says that, despite their age, their love was powerful.

Page 84
A Vocabulary
Possible answer: The love he and Annabel Lee shared.

Page 85
B Read and Discuss
To reinforce the love that these two young people shared and the depth that the narrator feels that love goes: **What does the speaker mean when he says nothing could ever "dissever," or separate, his soul from the soul of Annabel Lee?** Possible response: Although they are separated physically, their love is so deep that their souls will forever be connected.

D Reading Focus
Possible answer: In "User Friendly" and in "Annabel Lee," the main character experiences loneliness and longs for love. In "User Friendly," Kevin is lonely and longs for Ginny to love him, and he also longs for a friend. In "Annabel Lee," Poe longs for his departed Annabel, whom he loved so much. In both stories, the main character experiences tragic loss, only for Kevin, he loses his computer who was his only friend, and for Poe, he lost the love of his life to a terrible sickness.

Page 86
Skills Practice
Use a Concept Map
Possible answers:
1. "And this maiden she lived with no other thought than to love and be loved by me." (lines 5–6).
2. "But we loved with a love that was more than love" (line 9).
3. "The angels, not half so happy in heaven, went envying her and me" (lines 21–22).
4. "But our love it was stronger by far than the love of those who were older than we" (lines 27–28).
5. "For the moon never beams, without bringing me dreams of the beautiful Annabel Lee." (lines 34–35).
6. "…I lie down by the side of my darling— my darling—my life and my bride" (lines 38–39).

Page 87
Applying Your Skills
Comprehension Wrap Up
1. Possible response: The mood is sad but strong as the speaker misses his love but knows that they are forever connected. The speaker makes their love seem as epic as he says it is by using planetary imagery and language to create something colossal: "the moon never beams" (line 34), "the stars never rise" (line 36), etc.

Literary Focus
1. Students' answers will vary, but should support their stance on the question about poetry and the theme of loss.
2. Student's answers will vary, but should express how the poem made them feel.

Reading Focus
Possible answer: The themes in "User Friendly" and "Annabel Lee" were love, loss, and loneliness. In these selections, we see how strong the power of love can be. In "User Friendly," Kevin gets really hurt when Ginny does not reciprocate his feelings for her, and he is also deeply saddened when he finds out that his old computer, Louis, was really a girl computer—Louise—who had loved him, but it was too late because his dad had already pulled the plug on 'her.' In "Annabel Lee," the speaker's love for Annabel is so powerful that he thinks the only reason she died was because the angels were jealous of how strong their love was. He is lonely without her, but he still feels that their spirits are forever connected.

Vocabulary Review
1. Kinsmen   2. sepulcher

VIRTUAL STICKS AND STONES

Major Understanding for Read and Discuss Queries: This essay explores the "wild west" that is the internet of today. It illustrates the power of words when the reader may never see the writer and the way this type of relationship gives people the confidence to record thoughts they never would if their audience was right in front of them.

Page 89

B Read and Discuss
To set up that computer and internet use can have good and bad consequences—but either way it's a powerful set of tools: **How has Katie handled her experience?** Possible response: She turned the bad experience into a position of power, as she now helps others who are new to using the internet to deal with cyberbullying.

C Reading Focus
Possible answer: These facts provide strong evidence for the author's argument.

Page 90
A Read and Discuss
To recognize the author's point that it may be easier to "cyberbully" than it would to bully someone in person, and that communications through email can be easily misunderstood: **What does the author mean by "If you're in school and someone calls you a name, you can turn to him or her"?** Possible response: The author is saying that it seems extremely easy to write horrible things about people, because that means you don't have to be face-to-face with them when you hurt their feelings. **Follow-up: How is this different than cyberbullying?** Possible response: Being face to face also allows the person on the receiving end of a "joke" or "harmless ribbing" to pick up on the originator's intention by seeing their facial expressions and hearing the tone of voice.

Comprehension Wrap-Up
Possible responses:

1. Pretending in this fashion allows people to do things they would not normally do to others in person. These people can do things anonymously on the Internet, and can hide behind their computer personalities.
2. The phrase "sticks and stones may break my bones but words will never hurt me" is referred to in this title. Instead of spoken words, the title is referring to virtual words and the affects they can have on people.

Page 91
Applying Your Skills
Informational Text Focus
1. D

Possible answers:
1. Topic/subject: Cyberbullying
2. Writer's POV: Cyberbullying is common and very harmful, and people need to be careful of bullying and make sure to not bully others online.
3. Evidence: Numbers from a study and from a survey; the fact that many schools have Internet policies.

Possible argument: The author's argument is that cyberbullying is a serious and common problem among Internet users, and people need to be more aware of the issue.

Vocabulary Review
1. bully   2. symbol

SKILLS REVIEW

Page 92
Vocabulary Review
1. e   6. g
2. a   7. f
3. b   8. i
4. c   9. j
5. d   10. h

Students' sentences will vary, but should correctly include three of the vocabulary words used in the above activity.

Page 93
Language Coach
Possible answers:

1. The quiet boy did not make a sound; The boy moved quietly through the hall, never making a sound.
2. The quick girl beat the race in record timing; The girl ran the race quickly, setting a new record.
3. The crazy colors and designs of the bedspread made me dizzy!; The crazily designed bedspread was fascinating but dizzying!

Oral Language Activity
Students' answers will vary, but students should partner up and prepare a brief talk stating their opinions about an issue important to them, using at least two of the phrases provided.

Collection 5

NAMES/NOMBRES

Major Understanding for Read and Discuss Queries: A young girl struggles to fit into a new culture and learns to accept and be proud of her given name, as well as the American names bestowed upon her.

Page 97
A Read and Discuss
To establish that the Elbures family has just immigrated to New York City: **What have we learned about the "Elbures" family?**
Possible response: The Alvarez family just immigrated to New York City, and the immigration officer is having trouble pronouncing their name.

Page 98
C Read and Discuss
To elicit that Judy's mother also was embarrassed by the family's Spanish names: **What does the story about Mauricia's name tell you about the mother?** Possible response: Initially, Judy's mother was embarrassed by her daughter's Spanish sounding name and did not want to admit the name to the American mothers.

Page 99
D Reading Focus

Possible answer: Names are very important in shaping identity.

E Literary Focus
Possible answer: This author is sometimes objective and just reports facts. Other times, the author is subjective and inserts her own opinion.

F Vocabulary
Originally means "at first."

G Read and Discuss
To recognize that Julia's early years were trying, as she was embarrassed to be the "foreigner": **How does this information add to what we know about Julia and her early years in school?** Possible response: During her early years in school, she struggled with fitting in and didn't like being singled out as different.

Page 100
A Reading Focus
Possible answers: circle: "My different background was really clear when my whole family attended school events"/ "they spoke loudly among themselves."

B Read and Discuss
To highlight the strong bond between Julia and her extended family: **What does the fact that Julia's whole family comes to school events say about her family?** Possible response: They are a very close family and are proud of Julia's accomplishments.

D Read and Discuss
To establish that Julia now looks back on her many names with fond memories: **Julia laughs when she thinks about which "well known" name she would go by. What does this tell you about her?** Possible response: Although Julia was frustrated numerous times by people mispronouncing her name and inventing new ones for her, she is now able to look back on those times and laugh about them.

Comprehension Wrap-Up
1. Possible response: Julia learns she still loves her family members, despite all of their oddities. She learns also that family always takes precedence over friends.

Page 101

Applying Your Skills
Literary Focus
1. objective
2. subjective
3. objective

Reading Focus
Possible answers:
Main idea: Names are an important part of shaping identity.
Detail: When Julia's friends call her "Judy Alcatraz," she feels rebellious.
Detail: Because Julia's sister Ana has an American-sounding name, she adapts to American culture easily.
Detail: Julia's family pronounces her name with a Spanish intonation, which connects her to her heritage.

Vocabulary Review
1. homesick   2. Originally   3. declare

FROM BARRIO BOY

Major Understanding for Read and Discuss Queries: Ernesto and the other students at Lincoln School take a journey that provides them with classroom knowledge and teaches them about life.

Page 103
B Read and Discuss
To establish that Ernesto, a Spanish boy, is enrolling in a new school that is probably American: **What has the author told us so far?** Possible response: A boy named Ernesto, who is Spanish, is enrolling in a new school that is American.

Page 104
A Read and Discuss
To draw attention to the idea that although Ernesto thinks the principal is pretty nice, he isn't sure because she speaks only English and he can't understand her: **How are things going for Ernesto?** Possible response: He and his mother are meeting with the principal, and he thinks the principal seems to be a nice lady, but because he doesn't speak any English, he doesn't understand what she's saying.

B Read and Discuss
To understand that the other children in Ernesto's classroom are also from other countries and that his teacher seems to be

supportive of their progress: **What have we learned about Ernesto's class?** Possible response: All of the children are from various countries **Follow up: What have we learned about their teacher?** Possible response: She seems to be very patient with them and supportive of their progress.

Page 105
D Reading Focus
Possible answer: Ernesto is from Mexico and starts first grade in the United States; his new school is very helpful with his learning English; he finishes first grade with honors and loves his teacher.

E Vocabulary
Culture means "the beliefs and traditions of one's country."

F Read and Discuss
To reinforce that although the people at Ernesto's school tried very hard to teach the students English and help them become proud Americans, they never wanted them to lose sight of their individual cultures: **How does this new information connect with what we have already talked about?** Possible response: The teachers at Ernesto's school want the students to learn English and become Americans, but they also want the children to be proud of their different cultural backgrounds.

Page 106
Skills Practice
Use an Organization Map
Students' answers will vary, but should include the most important information in Ernesto's story.

Page 107
Applying Your Skills
Comprehension Wrap-Up
1. Possible response: Attending Lincoln School is a pivotal moment in Ernesto's life. Doing so allows him to embrace American culture while retaining his own roots.

Reading Focus
Students' answers will vary, but students' writing should reflect the information they organized while reading the story.

Vocabulary Review

1. culture   2. autobiography
3. pasture

CANINES TO THE RESCUE

Major Understanding for Read and Discuss Queries: This essay highlights the impressive behavior of rescue dogs. It also presents opposing theories regarding why dogs perform in such brave ways on behalf of their owners and others who need their help.

Page 109
B Read and Discuss
To begin to establish the extraordinary skill of dogs that are trained to locate people and objects: **What is the author showing us about dogs?** Possible Response: Dogs are especially gifted at finding bombs.

C Read and Discuss
To explore the idea that there is an emotional impact on dogs if they don't find people alive: **What does it mean that it is hard for dogs when they find bodies?** Possible Response: The dogs pick up on their owner's disappointment when bodies are found instead of survivors, and the dogs can become depressed as well as the men who care for them.

Page 110
C Reading Focus
Possible answer: The author thinks dogs are brave and heroic. They have their own instincts, but they also want to please people. The author thinks that it is more important to appreciate what dogs do for us than to worry about why they do it.

Comprehension Wrap-Up
1. Possible response: Heroic dogs like Servus are truly wonderful and deserve to be praised. It is good that the people working with Servus cared for him like a fellow human being and wanted him to get rest after his ordeal, but Servus's eagerness to get back to work just further demonstrates how amazing he is.

Page 111
Applying Your Skills
Informational Text Focus
1. A   2. B

Possible answers:

1. "But dogs love us as much as we love them" (line 40). This shows the author does not believe in the theory that dogs use us for their gain, but rather genuinely love us as we love them.

2. "Tara, the golden retriever, doesn't know she is looking for bombs. But she knows that she wants to please her human master. And isn't that good enough?" (lines 50-53). This shows that the author believes you should focus more on the great jobs dogs are doing rather than on why they do it.

Vocabulary Review
1. canines   2. ethic   3. survivors

SKILLS REVIEW

Page 112
Vocabulary Review
1. survivors   2. culture   3. ethic
4. homesick   5. declare   6. ambiguous

Students' sentences will vary, but should reflect an understanding of the vocabulary words.

Page 113
Language Coach
1. helpful   2. thankful   3. thoughtful

Students' sentences will vary, but should reflect an understanding of the words.

Writing Activity
Students' answers will vary, but should reflect an understanding of the selected stories and the notion of author's perspective.

Collection 6

CASTING CALL

Page 116
Preparing to Read
Reading Focus
Possible question: Who is making this movie?

Major Understanding for Read and Discuss Queries: Students should understand the purpose and importance of public documents, as well as have an understanding of how to interpret and respond to them. Specifically, students will develop that understanding by following one young lady, Sam, as she responds to just such a document.

Page 117
A Reading Focus
Possible answer: This is the most important information to remember.

B Read and Discuss
What do we know about this casting call?
Possible response: StreetWheelie Productions is looking for people to be in an action movie.

Comprehension Wrap-Up
1. Possible response: He or she would need to be cool, have bike skills, and look between 12 and 15 years old.

Page 118
Skills Practice
Use a Concept Map
Possible answers:
1. StreetWheelie Productions is looking for bikers for an action movie.
2. The audition is on May 25, 2004.
3. You need a work permit to work in California if you are younger than eighteen.

Page 119
Applying Your Skills
Informational Text Focus
1. D   2. C

Reading Focus
Students' answers will vary depending on the questions they asked on the Preparing to Read page.

Vocabulary Review
1. permit   2. audition

LETTER FROM CASTING DIRECTOR

Major Understanding for Read and Discuss Queries: Students should recognize that Sam was offered a part in the movie and also

*should understand the purpose of the
information provided in Sam's letter from the
casting director.*

Page 121
B Reading Focus
Possible answer: The most important information on the page comes under the heading "Your Responsibilities," because the list that follows tells Sam what she needs to do.

Page 122
A Vocabulary
Responsibilities means "things that one must do."

C Read and Discuss
To establish that Sam was offered a part in the movie but now she must accept the conditions as spelled out in the casting director's letter: **What is the purpose of this letter?** Possible response: The casting director provided specific guidelines—she must report two hours before her call time, she must check her e-mail, etc.—that Sam must agree to follow before she accepts the role in the movie.

Comprehension Wrap-Up
1. Possible response: These rules and responsibilities seem fairly straightforward, so it is likely that Samantha will be able to follow them.

Page 123
Applying Your Skills
Informational Text Focus
1. "Dear"
2. The business letter explains what Sam is agreeing to when she signs the contract.
3. The return address is listed at the top of the letter, above the date.

Reading Focus
Possible answer: After previewing this letter, it seems the first few sentences and the list of responsibilities are the most important. These indicate that a position has been offered, and they specify what that position requires.

Vocabulary Review
1. responsibilities
2. wage
3. arrival

BART MAP

casting director.

*Major Understanding for Read and Discuss
Queries: Students should understand that by
looking at the map, Sam discovered that BART
takes her directly from Walnut Creek to the
Embarcadero station.*

Page 125
B Vocabulary
Possible answer: The BART system is called a *network* because it consists of many different lines that are all connected.

C Read and Discuss
To establish that from looking at the BART System Map, Sam learned that BART will take her directly from Walnut Creek to the Embarcadero station: **Where is Sam starting and where does she want to go?** Possible response: BART will take her directly from Walnut Creek to the Embarcadero station.

Page 126
A Reading Focus
Possible answer: This graphic aid shows the BART System Map—where all of the lines run and where the stops are.

C Read and Discuss
What has Sam learned from the BART System Map? Possible response: She is thrilled that she can get to where she needs to go.

Page 127
Applying Your Skills
Comprehension Wrap-Up
1. Possible response: Maps help us get where we need to go so that we can save time and not have to worry about getting lost all the time. Maps are extremely useful in this way. They can help us plan trips or assist us in showing others how to get places.

Informational Text Focus
Possible answer: Sam could have bought a map somewhere, or asked someone if they knew the directions.

Reading Focus
1. B   2. A

Vocabulary Review

Holt Adapted Reader Answer Key

1. evacuation 2. accommodate
3. deducted

HOW TO CHANGE A FLAT TIRE

Major Understanding for Read and Discuss Queries: This article walks the reader through the simple process of changing a tire, but offers cautionary tips to ensure the safety of those changing the tire.

Page 129
B Read and Discuss
To recognize some of the ways to determine whether a tire is flat: **What has the author set up for us in this paragraph?** Possible response: The author gives us several ways we might determine if a tire is flat.

Page 130
A Vocabulary
Remove means "take off."

B Vocabulary
Counterclockwise means "in the direction opposite of the movement of the hands of a clock."

D Read and Discuss
To establish that changing a tire is relatively simple, though it's imperative that people follow the directions or it could turn dangerous: **Why does the author include this warning?** Possible response: The warnings indicate that although this procedure is fairly simple, it could be dangerous if we aren't careful to follow all of the cautionary instructions.

Page 131
F Reading Focus
Students' answers will vary, but might include hooking up a DVD player, wrapping a sprained ankle with an elastic bandage, or assembling a bookcase.

Page 132

Skills Practice
Use a Sequencing Table
Possible answers:
Step 4: Loose the lug nuts, usually by turning them counterclockwise.

Step 5: Consult your owner's manual to position your car jack.
Step 6: Use the jack to lift the car until the flat tire is two or three inches off the ground.
Step 7: Finish unscrewing the lug nuts and place them inside the wheel cover.
Step 8: Remove the flat tire, replace it with the spare tire, and tighten the lug nuts by hand.
Step 9: Lower the car and remove the jack. Then tighten the lug nuts with the lug wrench.
Step 10: Place the flat tire and tools in the trunk. Buy a new tire to replace the spare, so you can keep your spare tire for emergencies.

Page 133
Applying Your Skills
Comprehension Wrap-Up
1. Possible response: Step 9 might be considered the most important, because it tells you how and when to tighten the different lug nuts. This is important so that the spare tire will stay in place after you put it on. Skipping this step could result in disaster.

Informational Text Focus
Students' answers will vary depending on the technical devices they choose, but should include the correct steps to operate the chosen device.

Reading Focus
Possible answers:
1. There are ten steps required to change a flat tire.
2. You should keep the unscrewed lug nuts in the wheel cover so you don't lose them.

Vocabulary Review
1. standard 2. procedures

TILTING AT WINDMILLS

Major Understanding for Read and Discuss Queries: The students will understand that the wind is a renewable source that generates electricity. The article also conveys some of the arguments for and against wind's usage.

Page 135
A Read and Discuss
To draw attention to the need for an alternative to fossil fuels: **What are the problems with fossil fuels?** Possible

Holt Adapted Reader Answer Key

response: Burning fossil fuels to create electricity puts harmful pollutants into the air. In addition to the dangers of these substances, fossil fuels are running out, so other cleaner, available power sources are being investigated.

Page 136
A Reading Focus
Possible answer: An oil shortage and rising fuel prices caused people to build wind farms.

C Read and Discuss
To emphasize some advantages of windmills: **What's the writer's point here?** Possible response: Windmills generate electricity in a way that's clean and doesn't rely on fossil fuels. So far, Germany, Spain, and the U.S. are the top producers of wind power, so the results show that wind power works.

Page 137
E Reading Focus
Possible answer: The desired effect of wind power is for people to meet their energy needs without polluting the atmosphere or using up natural resources.

Comprehension Wrap-Up
1. Possible response: Windmills have been able to pump and move water, pound grain, turn wheels, and create other kinds of power. Modern windmills create electricity, making people rely less on fossil fuels, which can harm the air. Windmills do not use up natural resources or pollute the air.

Page 138
Skills Practice
Use a Chain of Events Chart
Possible answers:
1. Cause: Fossil fuels are burnt for energy.
2. Effect: That energy allows us to power lights, computers, and other electric devices.
3. Effect: Burning fossil fuels also releases harmful substances into the air.

Page 139
Applying Your Skills
Reading Focus
1. A   2. D

Students' answers will vary, but may indicate that fossil fuels create electricity, but they can

release harmful pollutants and also run out. Windmills can create power naturally, and wind can never run out or pollute.

Vocabulary Review
1. generate   2. pollution   3. limited

SKILLS REVIEW

Page 140
Vocabulary Review
1. c   2. a
3. d   4. b

Students' sentences will vary, but should reflect an understanding of each vocabulary word.

Page 141
Language Coach
Students' answers will vary, but should resemble the following possible answers:
1. I took the red line from South Station to Quincy Center.
2. My teacher drew a line through my story's title and suggested that I change it.
3. We waited in line for concert tickets for two hours.

Oral Language Activity
Students' answers will vary, but students should describe a series of logical steps to accomplish an everyday task.

Collection 7

I'M NOBODY!

Major Understanding for Read and Discuss Queries: The poet declares that she is Nobody and then seems delighted to have found another Nobody. She then gives commentary on how dreadful it must be to be Somebody allowing the reader to question whether the poet sincerely thinks it would be dreary to be Somebody, or if she is speaking from a jealous place in her heart.

Page 145
A Read and Discuss

To establish that the poet claims that she is Nobody and appears to be happy about finding another Nobody: **What has the poet told you so far?** Possible response: She says she is Nobody, and she has found someone else who is Nobody. **Follow-up: Why does she say that they cannot tell anyone they are Nobodies?** Allow students to play with the idea that the poet is trying to convince either herself or her friend that they are special because they are Nobodies.

C Language Coach
The speaker compares a "somebody" to a frog.

Comprehension Wrap-Up
1. Possible response: She would rather be Nobody; being Somebody is too public.

Page 146
Skills Practice
Use a Question and Answer Chart
Possible answers:
Answer Box: She means that she is not famous and not important in the public sphere.
Question Box: Who is Dickinson talking to?
Answer Box: Another person who is removed from the public sphere, just like her.
Question Box: Why does Dickinson think it would be "dreary to be Somebody"?
Answer Box: Because she wouldn't feel comfortable being judged and hassled by everyone.

Page 147
Applying Your Skills
Literary Focus
1. Possible answer: The poet does not seem to like people who look up to celebrities. A bog is not a pleasant place, and she does not describe the creatures as being smart or interesting. They just want to listen to a frog croak, just as people will listen to anything that anybody famous says.

Reading Focus
Possible answer: Asking yourself questions about the text of a poem as you read can help you break the poem down into bits-and-pieces which are easier to understand. It can be very easy to miss important things in a poem if you don't stop to make sure you understand them. You become more engaged in your reading when you examine words more closely. And you have a better chance of realizing the author's intended message if you take time to analyze their work.

Vocabulary Development
1. No   2. Yes   3. Yes

THE RUNAWAY

Major Understanding for Read and Discuss Queries: The poet writes about seeing a colt that seems baffled and frightened by the snow, as the winter is a new experience for it. The question is raised about who is keeping an eye on this colt.

Page 149

B Read and Discuss
To introduce the skittish colt in the pasture: **What has the poet told us about the colt?** No one seems to recognize the young horse in the pasture as it darts about and runs away. It appears frightened by the snow—not just playful.

Page 150
A Literary Focus
The rhyme scheme is a/a; yes. The two words that rhyme in these lines are "bin" and "in."

C Read and Discuss
To draw attention to the needs of the colt: **What happens at the end of the poem?** Neither the mother nor the owner seems to be tending to the frightened colt, and it's a concern.

Comprehension Wrap-Up:
1. Possible response: During the course of the poem, the colt runs away.

Page 151
Applying Your Skills
Literary Focus
a/a/b/c/b/c/d/d

Reading Focus
Students should practice reading the poem aloud, paying close attention to punctuation as they go along. When they are comfortable with the poem, students can read the poem to the class.

Vocabulary Review

Students' sentences will vary, but should reflect an understating of the poem and should correctly use each vocabulary word.

SKILLS REVIEW

Page 152
Vocabulary Review
 1. mounts 2. admiring 3. comment
 4. colt 5. tradition 6. vision

Students' sentences will vary, but should reflect an understanding of each vocabulary word.

Page 153
Language Coach
 1. metaphor 2. simile 3. simile
 4. metaphor 5. simile

Oral Language Activity
Students should practice reading one of the poems from this collection aloud, paying close attention to punctuation as they go along. When they are comfortable with the poem, students may read the poem to the class.

Collection 8

THE MONSTERS ARE DUE ON MAPLE STREET

Major Understanding for Read and Discuss Queries: Set in the Twilight Zone, this is a science fiction play by Rod Serling that examines how easily someone can be maligned and how one person, even a child, can trigger irrational mob emotion and the search for a scapegoat.

Page 158
B Read and Discuss
To establish the narrator's explanation that this story comes from the realm of the Twilight Zone: **What is the narrator sharing with you?** Possible response: The narrator is telling us that there is a 5th dimension, the imagination, which is beyond man's knowledge. This story is from the Twilight Zone.

Page 159
D Read and Discuss
To set up both the ordinariness of this small town and the characters of Steve and Don: **What is this all about?** Possible response: Maple Street in the late summer is just a quiet small town with people relaxing or doing outdoor chores. **Follow-up: What did you learn from the conversation between Steve and Don?** Possible response: The men discuss a huge screeching sound and a flash of light in the sky that caused them to stop what they were doing.

Page 160
B Literary Focus
Possible answer: Not even the portable radio works, which should not be affected by the power outage.

Page 161

D Read and Discuss
To draw attention to the neighborhood's loss of power and probable reason: **What has happened?** Possible response: All the neighbors are realizing and then talking about not having electricity. It's strange that even phones, cars, and portable radios are not working as well. **Follow up: How does everything stopping connect to the narrator's comment?** Possible response: One minute after the sound and the flash, the narrator says this is the calm before the monsters came. So apparently that's the reason everything stopped working.

Page 162
A Vocabulary
Intimidated means "frightened."

B Literary Focus
There is now the possibility that the power outage was caused by a ship from outer space.

C Read and Discuss
To acknowledge Tommy's idea that those from outer space are in control: **What does this show you about Tommy?** Possible response: Fourteen year old Tommy's idea seems foolish and juvenile at first and the adults explain that the power problems could be due to meteors or to sunspots or to anything but to that flashing light that carried "them" in a space ship to Maple Street.

Page 163
D Vocabulary
Possible answer: Tommy is feeling equally scared and bold.

Page 164
C Read and Discuss
To underscore that Tommy is adamant about Steve Brand not leaving because he's not part of those who were sent ahead of the spacecraft: **What is on Tommy's mind?** Possible response: Because of the story that Tommy knows of, he insists that Steve not leave. In fact, the only people who can leave, according to Tommy, are those emissaries who look like humans and have been sent ahead. **Follow-up: How are the neighbors reacting to Tommy's idea?** Possible response: Steve is skeptical but asks Tommy questions. Another neighbor says it's crazy talk, but the tone is changing. Charlie changes the subject, asking about Pete Van Horn.

Page 165
D Literary Focus
Possible answer: The characters are left to hope and wonder about what is going on elsewhere, leaving them even more confused.

Page 166
A Vocabulary
Metamorphosis means "change of form."

Page 167
B Literary Focus
Possible answer: Mr. Goodman looks like he might have something to do with the situation, and it makes the others distrust him.

Page 168
B Read and Discuss
To focus on the turn against Les Goodman and aligning him with "the thing": **What is the author getting at?** Possible response: The neighbors are suspicious of Les now because his car started on its own and yet nothing else is working. They think he must be connected to "them." The author says, "their fear almost turned their walk into a wild stampede." The neighbors' fear is being turned against Les.

Page 169
Applying Your Skills
Literary Focus

Possible answer: At the beginning of Act One, the characters want to know about the meteor they think landed and about why the power has gone out. At the end, everyone wants to know how Goodman is involved with everything.

Reading Focus
Possible answers:
Purpose*:* To entertain people./ Evidence: This is a script written for TV.
Purpose: To make people think about how quickly we are to blame others./ Evidence: Everyone jumps to the conclusion at the end that Mr. Goodman has something to do with the problem and don't seem to believe him.

Vocabulary Development
1. transfixed   2. intimidated
3. inexplicably

Page 170
A Vocabulary
Here, *blankets* means "covers completely."

Page 171
B Vocabulary
Sally's tone here is fearful.

Page 172
B Reading Focus
Possible answer: The author's purpose for having Steve say this is to show just how ridiculous the situation has become.

Page 173
C Literary Focus
People are suspicious of the ham radio Steve has.

D Reading Focus
Possible answer: People are quick to blame others when trouble arises, instead of working together to solve problems.

E Read and Discuss
To recognize the increased tension, the neighbors act like a surveillance group, the Goodman family is extremely tense, and Charlie and Steve are snarling at each other: **What can you say about the neighbors now?** Possible response: Most are wary of the Goodmans and Charlie seems to go after Les Goodman and Steve, too. Steve calls Charlie a "hanging judge," sentencing without sufficient evidence and Don attacks Steve because Steve

has a ham radio. All are snipping at each other about things that don't seem important or rational.

Page 174
B Read and Discuss
To understand that Pete Van Horn has been shot by Charlie because of the growing desperation and fears of the crowd: **What is going on?** Possible response: Tommy talks about the monster and Don has a gun for protection. Steve tries to calm the group but Charlie snatches the gun and shoots the dark figure, Pete.

Page 175
C Reading Focus
Possible answer: To continue to show how frightened and crazy people have become.

D Literary Focus
Possible answer: Now, people are suspecting that Charlie may have had something to do with the power outage because he shot Pete, and because his lights have just come on.

Page 176
A Vocabulary
Possible answer: The crowd is closing in on the porch.

B Reading Focus
Possible answers: Charlie is desperate to blame anyone else to get himself out of trouble; the people are convinced that the situation can be resolved by finding someone to blame.

Page 177
C Literary Focus
Possible answer: Everything has gone totally out of control; people are completely confused, violent, and they no longer trust each other.

Page 178
A Read and Discuss
To emphasize the turn of events because Charlie's house lights up and everything else is in the dark: **Now what is developing?** Possible response: Charlie is thought to be favored by "them" because now his house is lit and the crowd chases Charlie and throws rocks at him. Then Charlie says "it" is really Tommy. Panic ensues as Tommy, Charlie, Steve, Les, Bob and Don are all accused as

lights in their houses go on and off. A spacecraft opens with two figures appearing.

B Vocabulary
"vague"

Page 179
C Read and Discuss
To appreciate the irony of this attack—we destroy ourselves: **So how does the teleplay end?** Possible response: The attackers didn't even have to attack directly, but got the humans to become suspicious and attack each other. "They" had this all planned by just stopping the humans' power source, putting them in darkness for a short time and then the human prejudices took charge.

D Reading Focus
Possible answer: What happened on the fictitious Maple Street can and does happen all the time in real life, but in different ways.

Comprehension Wrap-Up
1. Possible response: The horrors of the Holocaust stemmed from the hatred and prejudices of Adolf Hitler and his poisonous rhetoric; Senator Joseph McCarthy's suspicions and unsubstantiated claims of so-called "Communists" led to Senate hearings and a witch hunt of innocent American citizens.

Page 180
Skills Practice
Use a Chain of Events Chart
Students' answers will vary, but should indicate and summarize three major plot complications in the order they occurred.

Page 181
Applying Your Skills
Literary Focus
Students' answers will vary but should include events such as the power going out, certain people's cars and electricity suddenly working, people suspecting and blaming one another, Pete getting shot, and people breaking out into violence at the end.

Reading Focus
Students' answers will vary, but may indicate the idea that prejudice, suspicion, and mistrust can sometimes harm us more than weapons.

Holt Adapted Reader Answer Key

Vocabulary Review
1. timorously 2. menace
3. materialized

SKILLS REVIEW

Page 182
Vocabulary Review
1. yes 2. yes 3. no
4. yes 5. yes 6. yes

Students' sentences will vary, but should reflect an understanding of each vocabulary word.

Page 183
Language Coach
1. Circle: "un"; changes the meaning from to "not intelligent."
2. Circle "pre"; changes the meaning to "view before."
3. Circle "dis"; changes the meaning to "not in agreement."
4. Circle "in"; changes the meaning to "not experienced."
5. Circle "over"; Changes the meaning to "react excessively."

Oral Language Activity
Students should read the teleplay aloud and note stage directions as they go.

Collection 9

ORPHEUS, THE GREAT MUSICIAN

Major Understanding for Read and Discuss Queries: This myth explores the range of emotions love and loss can cause and how those two experiences influence the singing of Orpheus.

Page 187
A Read and Discuss
To establish that Orpheus was such a talented musician that when he sang, all of nature was affected: **What does this information about wild beasts, trees, and gods tell us about Orpheus?** Possible response: Orpheus is so good at singing that everything around him—

inanimate or not—seems to inch closer, come to life or become tamed by his great music.

Page 188
A Literary Focus
Possible answer: The underworld is below the ground. There is a path leading down there. There are ghosts and monsters, but Orpheus quiets them with his music.

C Reading Focus
Possible answer: Underline: "He worried…bride"/ "Quickly he turned"/ "the shadow disappeared."

Comprehension Wrap-Up
1. Possible response: Orpheus's singing changes in that he once sang beautiful songs of love. However, now that Orpheus lost the chance to be with Eurydice, his songs are sad.

Page 189
Applying Your Skills
Literary Focus
Students' answers will vary but may indicate that the ancient Greeks believed that people's souls lived on in the underworld. Based on this story, the underworld seems dark and frightening because of the ghosts and monsters that roam there.

Reading Focus
Possible answers:
Title: Orpheus, the Great Musician
Author: Unknown, retold by Olivia Coolidge
Main Character: Orpheus
Main Events: Eurydice dies, Orpheus goes to the underworld to save her, he convinces Hades to let her go, and when he turns around he loses her until he is killed and reunited with her in the underworld.
Summary: "Orpheus, the Great Musician" is about a great musician named Orpheus. His wife Eurydice dies and Orpheus goes to the underworld to bring her back. The god of the underworld, Hades, says that Orpheus cannot look at her on his journey out of the underworld. They walk back above ground, but at the last minute, Orpheus turns around and looks at her, so Eurydice disappears. Orpheus is sad until he dies, when they can be finally be together again in the underworld.

Vocabulary Review
1. comforted 2. spell 3. unmoved

Holt Adapted Reader Answer Key

Page 190
Vocabulary Review
Possible answers:
1. unemotional 2. relieved
3. charm   4. traditional
5. basis   6. era
7. interrupt

Students' sentences will vary, but should reflect an understanding of each vocabulary word.

Page 191
Language Coach
Possible answers:
1. Underline: "un"; changes the meaning of the word from "moved" to "not moved."
2. Underline: "tion"; changes the meaning of the word from "started" to "a beginning or basis for something else."
3. Underline "inter"; The prefix *inter-* means "between or among," so "intervene" means to get between something to stop something else from happening.

Oral Language Activity
Students' speeches will vary, but should be convincing and demonstrate an understanding of what Orpheus is asking of Hades.

Second Course

Collection 1

THE TREASURE OF LEMON BROWN

Major Understanding for Read and Discuss Queries: Greg's poor math grades provoke dad's lectures and refusal to allow his son to join the prized basketball team. But instead of studying, Greg investigates a vacant building and meets Lemon Brown, a man who teaches Greg about the meaning of a father's legacy and a son's respect for that gift. Greg returns home with a greater understanding about what dad is truly offering him.

Page 3
B Read and Discuss
To establish that the father/son confrontation is due to Greg's not studying and the resulting poor math grades: **How is the story starting off?** Possible response: Dad insists his son needs to spend more time studying math, not playing basketball.

Page 4
C Literary Focus
Possible answer: Greg is relaxed because he recognizes the man as someone he has seen before, picking through the trash.

Page 5
D Read and Discuss
To draw attention to Greg and Lemon Brown's meeting, questioning, and talking with one another: **What is all this telling us?** Possible response: Greg finds Lemon Brown in the vacant building and they size up one another. They seem at ease with one another and talk. Lemon explains that he was a blues singer who's down on his luck. **Follow-up: What do you make of the boy's response when asked why he's there?** Possible response: Greg turns away, answers briefly and probably doesn't want to talk about why he doesn't want to be at home. It's not the most logical place to be; perhaps Lemon thinks the boy is in trouble.

Page 6
B Reading Focus
Possible answer: Greg and Lemon try to scare the men. Greg howls while Lemon Brown stands at the top of the stairs, his shadow looming eerily.

C Read and Discuss
To emphasize that the poor old man does have a treasure to protect, his keepsake fifty-year-old newspaper articles about his musical performances and his battered harmonica: **What have we learned about Lemon Brown's treasure now?** Possible response: Lemon's treasure, old newspaper reviews about his music and his old harmonica, are wrapped in plastic around his leg. These must be important to Lemon as he's kept them so long and so close to him.

Page 7
D Vocabulary
Circle: "dented badly"

E Reading Focus
Possible answer: Greg asks Lemon about his treasure, and if it was really worth fighting over. Lemon says yes, since all a man has are what he can pass on to his child. The two part ways.

F Read and Discuss
To appreciate the effect that Lemon Brown had on the change in Greg from the beginning of the story: **What has happened between the boy and the old man?** *Possible response: Greg and Lemon show concern for one another and wish each other well – Greg goes home and Lemon will be leaving the area.*

G Literary Focus
Students' answers will vary, but their opinions should be based on facts from the story.

Comprehension Wrap-Up
1. Possible response: Greg can become inspired by how his father made it in life and then know and learn how he can make it, as well.

Page 8
Skills Practice
Use a Concept Map
Possible answers:
1. His dad wants him to study harder and will not let him play basketball.

2. He comes across someone threatening him with a razor in the tenement.
3. He is nervous about the three men who come in.
4. He and Lemon Brown have to make the three men go away.

Page 9
Applying Your Skills
Literary Focus
Possible answers:
1. He has to face the three men taking his treasure, as well as the pain of having lost his son.
2. He wants to make sure Greg studies hard so he can have a good life, even if it means not letting him play basketball.

Reading Focus
1. b   2. c

Vocabulary Review
1. battered   2. eerie

THE INN OF LOST TIME

Major Understanding for Read and Discuss Queries: This is an illusive tale about ancient Japanese characters and events that are not what they seem. The detective work of an observant samurai unravels the mystery of lost time while readers, too, will consider the value of our earthly time.

Page 11
B Read and Discuss
To establish that two wandering, unemployed samurai were listening to a father tell a bedtime story to his three young boys: **What has the author set up so far?** Possible response: A father tells his three eager young children a bedtime story while his wife and two visitors listen. **Follow-up: What did we learn about the ronin?** Possible response: They are traveling soldiers looking for work. Typically, they defend the weak and serve an honorable code.

Page 12
A Vocabulary
Samurai as supposed to protect people who are weak or need help.

B Vocabulary

The author is sure that the boys have heard the story before.

C Vocabulary
Circle: (c)

Page 13
D Read and Discuss
To recognize the significance of Taro's reward in the children's bedtime story: **The father is telling a story. What happened on land while Taro was under the sea?** Possible response: Lonely in the undersea world of the princess, Taro returns home where time has been on "fast forward" and his family and most friends have died. Upset, he opens the forbidden box from the princess and instantly, he is very old. So the reward of life underwater with the princess is not something the man wanted and, in addition, he lost the most precious of human gifts – time.

Page 14
B Vocabulary
Possible answer: Zenta probably wants to say something polite to his hosts so they do not feel bad about not having much to offer.

D Read and Discuss
To emphasize that the adults discuss the value of time in our lives: **The adults are having a serious conversation. What do we learn about Zenta from this conversation?** *Possible response: When the adults talk over the story's tragedy—Taro's loss of family, friends, and time—Zenta, the older samurai, remembers someone he knew who was willing to pay one gold coin to regain each year lost.*

Page 15
F Vocabulary
Circle: "wealthy merchants are relatively new in our country"/ "Merchants, regarded as parasites"/ "despised class"

G Vocabulary
They saw merchants as bad people.

Page 16
B Vocabulary
Circle: "hungry"

Page 18
A Reading Focus

Holt Adapted Reader Answer Key

Underline: "The inn was peaceful and quiet";
"We were the only guests"; "I should have
been suspicious."

B Language Coach
cushions

Page 19
E Reading Focus
Possible answer: They are not innkeepers by
choice. The host was a samurai but had to turn
his house into an inn to make money.

G Read and Discuss
*To focus on Zenta's reminiscence of Tokubei,
the merchant:* **What is Zenta explaining?**
Possible response: Years ago, when Zenta was
merchant Tokubei's bodyguard, they stopped
at an inn and found the experience odd—the
girl with six fingers welcomed them, and no
other guests were present at the inn. **Follow-
up: How do the door panels connect to
Tokubei?** Possible response: The artwork on
the doors is beautiful, with different scenes on
left and right panels. Since Tokubei is a
merchant interested in valuable things to sell
to others and because the innkeeper seems to
need money, there may be a deal developing.

H Reading Focus
Underline: "Again I noticed her strange left
hand with its six fingers" or "The extra little
finger always stuck out from the hand".

Page 20
A Vocabulary
Possible answer: Zenta has been drugged, so
things look *blurry* before he passes out.

B Read and Discuss
*To acknowledge Tokubei and Zenta's
confusion as they try to reconcile their
previous experiences at the inn:* **What
happened?** Possible response: Both Tokubei
and Zenta awoke on the ground, are confused
and panicky especially when they see an old
woman with six fingers, a house, an
innkeeper, and door panels similar to but not
exactly like those they'd seen before.

D Reading Focus
Circle: "I got up shakily"/ "my head was
swimming"/ "I stumbled over to my
employer"

Page 21
F Literary Focus

Possible answer: The men are worried and
confused. The mood is one of confusion and
surprise as they try to figure out what
happened to them.

Page 22
B Literary Focus
Possible answer: The men are still worried.
Now the mood is more dangerous, as Zenta
reaches for his sword.

C Vocabulary
Circle: "Yes? she inquired."

D Reading Focus
Zenta sees the old woman's left hand with six
fingers.

Page 24
B Vocabulary
Circle: "played" and "joke"

D Reading Focus
Possible answer: The young girl could not
make her hands look twisted with arthritis.

Page 25
F Language Coach
suspicion

G Read and Discuss
*To acknowledge Tokubei and Zenta's
confusion as they try to reconcile their
previous experiences at the inn:* **What do the
men think has happened to them?** Possible
response: Both Tokubei and Zenta awoke on
the ground, were confused and panicky
especially when they saw an old woman with
six fingers, a house, an innkeeper, and door
panels similar but not exactly like those they'd
seen before.

H Vocabulary
Confirmed means "validated."

I Vocabulary
"Curse"; *Accursed* means "being under a
curse."

Page 26
A Vocabulary
Circle: (a)

B Reading Focus
Possible answer: Because Zenta traveled, he
did not have connections to family or business

Holt Adapted Reader Answer Key

like Tokubei. Zenta's sole purpose was to take care of his boss.

Page 27
E Read and Discuss
To understand that the lost fifty years can be regained through the intercession of the shrine priestess but at a high expense to Tokubei:
The man is talking about the powers of the shrine priestess. What is all this telling us?
Possible response: Tokubei and Zenta are realizing that while they've been at the inn, they've lost fifty years of time. Working through an expensive priestess, however, the merchant can buy back his time, one gold coin per year.

Page 28
A Reading Focus
Tokubei realizes that while at the inn, he and Zenta have lost fifty years.

B Vocabulary
Circle: (b)

Page 29
C Language Coach
"resigned"

D Literary Focus
Possible answer: No, the old woman does not seem understanding of Tokubei's problem. She laughs at him and is not sad that he has lost his wife. Her words reflect the turmoil that Tokubei and Zenta feel.

Page 30
B Vocabulary
Inconsistency means "variation; something that is not the same."

C Reading Focus
Possible answer: These details reinforce the idea that things are not as they seem, and suggest that Tokubei and Zenta's hosts have not been honest with them.

D Read and Discuss
To focus on the rational explanation behind the hoax: **Zenta seems to be realizing something about his experience. What is on Zenta's mind?** Possible response: Zenta spotted many inconsistencies – one day's bamboo growth, not fifty years growth; the panel paintings were different, not just older; the girl and the woman were two different

people each with six fingers, not one person who aged. The reason for the innkeeper's swindle was to make money from the merchant Tokubei.

Page 31
E Language Coach
whole

F Vocabulary
Underline: "mouth hung open"/ "his face became first red and then purple"/ "he turned furiously to me"/ the exclamation points.
Swindle means "trick" or "cheat."

Page 32
B Reading Focus
Underline: "The hand had six fingers."
Possible answer: The story Zenta told was true, and the farmer's wife was the young girl.

C Reading Focus
The old woman was her grandmother. The host was her brother.

Page 33
E Literary Focus
The farmers' house where Zenta and Matsuzo are staying is the same house where Zenta and Tobukei stayed.

Page 34
Skills Practice
Use a Venn Diagram
Students' Venn diagrams will vary, but should reflect what was similar and different on the first and second day of the tale.

Page 35
Applying Your Skills
Literary Focus
Circle:
  1. inn   **2.** forest
  3. morning   **4.** grove

Reading Focus
Students' answers will vary, but should include details from the story that help set the mood.

Vocabulary Review
desolate: lonely; miserable
poignant: emotionally painful
ruefully: with embarrassment
grueling: very tiring

traumatic: causing sadness or pain

PHYSICAL SCIENCE

Major Understanding for Read and Discuss Queries: This article should develop students' understanding of the scientific method, as it reviews the steps in the process, as well as provides an accompanying example of the method through Czarnowski and Triantafyllou's work.

Page 38
A Reading Focus
Behavior of Gases

Page 39
B Read and Discuss
To establish that the article is going to be about how scientists use scientific methods to answer questions, in particular, two men who studied penguins as a way to improve ships: **What is the author setting up for us?**
Possible response: The author is letting us know that the text is going to be about scientists and how they use scientific methods to answer questions. **Follow-up: How do James Czarnowski and Michael Triantafyllou fit into that equation?**
Possible response: They are two scientists who studied penguins in order to improve ships.

Page 40
A Vocabulary
Underline: "Observation is any use of the senses to gather information."

B Reading Focus
The heading reads "Asking a Question," and the subheading reads "Read-World Questions." This page will likely explain how scientists go about starting an experiment with a question and then proceed to make observations.

C Reading Focus
Figure 3 is a caption that gives the names of the people in the photos.

Page 41
D Read and Discuss
To draw attention to Czarnowski and Triantafyllou's important question: **Now what have we learned about Czarnowski and Triantafyllou?** Possible response: They were two scientists (a graduate student and his professor) who posed a question, "How can boat propulsion systems be made more efficient?" **Follow up: Why is this such an important question?** Possible response: Making a small percentage of boats just 10% more efficient would save millions of liters of fuel per year. **Follow up: How does their question fit in with our discussion of the scientific method?** Possible response: Their question is the first step in the scientific method.

Page 42
A Vocabulary
Possible answer: theory

B Read and Discuss
To identify two more steps in the scientific method, making predictions and testing the hypothesis: **How does this new information add to what we know about the scientific method?** Possible response: The next two steps are to make a prediction and then test the hypothesis. **Follow up: How do these steps fit in with the two men's hypothesis?** Possible response: *If* two flippers are attached to a boat, *then* the boat will be more efficient than a boat powered by propellers. The men would then have to test their hypothesis.

Page 43
Applying Your Skills
Informational Text Focus
1. A **2.** C **3.** C

Vocabulary Review
1. c **2.** a
3. b **4.** d

SKILLS REVIEW

Page 44
Vocabulary Review
1. b **2.** c **3.** a
4. e **5.** d **6.** g
7. f

Students' sentences will vary, but should reflect an understanding of each vocabulary word.

Page 45
Language Coach
Circle: "colonel"/ "scene"/ "campaign"/ "whole"

Writing Activity
Students' summaries will vary, but should follow the three steps given in the directions.

Collection 2

A RETRIEVED REFORMATION

Major Understanding for Read and Discuss Queries: A professional and very successful criminal, Jimmy, has a change of heart and decides to lead a "new" life. Jimmy's past life as a criminal and the knowledge he gained working as a safe cracker allow him to save a child's life and prompt others to see the new Jimmy.

Page 49
A Read and Discuss
To appreciate the playful conversation between Jimmy and the warden—the warden recognizing that Jimmy is a criminal and Jimmy adamantly denying it: **What does the conversation between Jimmy and the warden tell us about Jimmy?** Possible response: Apparently Jimmy's crime is safe cracking and the warden is letting Jimmy know he's on to him. We also find out that Jimmy might not be a bad guy despite his crimes.

Page 50
A Read and Discuss
To draw attention to the contents of Jimmy's suitcase and how that fits in with what we know about him: **How does this new information add to what we already know about Jimmy?** Possible response: Apparently, the warden was right—Jimmy was cracking safes. When he opens his suitcase in his room it is filled with all the tools needed to crack safes.

B Read and Discuss
To acknowledge that Jimmy is up to his old tricks—a series of safe crackings has been reported, and they seem to have Jimmy's safe cracking blueprint: **What is Jimmy up to now?** Possible response: Apparently, he's up to his old tricks—cracking safes, and the police suspect as much.

Page 51
E Read and Discuss
To further develop Jimmy's character and to establish that Jimmy has set off to a new town: **What is going on?** Possible response: Jimmy has traveled to a new town. **Follow-up: What do Jimmy's conversations with the people in Elmore tell us about him?** Possible response: Jimmy seems to be quite charming, as he is flirting a bit with a young woman and giving a young boy money. However, there's a reason he's being so charming—he's trying to find out information about the town.

Page 52
A Read and Discuss
To draw attention to Jimmy's "perfect life": **How are things looking for Jimmy?** Possible response: Pretty good. He has a successful shoe store, he's earned the respect of the community, and he's about to be married.

B Read and Discuss
To recognize that Jimmy has decided to give up the safe cracking business and live an honest life: **What does Jimmy's letter tell us?** Possible response: Jimmy has decided to give up his "old life" and live an honest one. He wants to meet with an old friend to turn over his special safe cracking tools.

Page 53
D Read and Discuss
To appreciate the suspenseful scene—Jimmy and his fiancée are in the bank with her sister's children, when one of the girls shuts the other in the bank vault. Meanwhile Ben Price is looking on: **What is going on?** Possible response: While Jimmy and his fiancée are in the bank with her sister, one of her children locks the other in the bank safe. The child and mother are in a panic, and no one seems to be able to open the safe. Meanwhile, Ben Price also has entered the bank and is watching the scene. **Follow-up: What mood has the author created for us?** Possible response: It's pretty suspenseful because the child is stuck in the safe, no one knows how to open it, and there stands Jimmy with the knowledge and the tools necessary to solve the problem.

Holt Adapted Reader Answer Key

E Reading Focus

Students' answers will vary, but should include a description of a movie or television show that reminds them of this story, as well as an explanation as to why it reminds them of this story.

Page 54
A Read and Discuss

To elicit that Jimmy drew upon his knowledge of safe cracking to save the little girl: **What does it mean that "Ralph D. Spencer passed away, and Jimmy Valentine took his place"?** Possible response: To the people of the town, Jimmy was Mr. Spencer, but Mr. Spencer wouldn't have been able to help the girl. Jimmy had to pull upon his past and become Jimmy the safe cracker in order to save the girl.

B Vocabulary

Students' answers will vary, but some students might think Jimmy has gone through a reformation because he has not really changed back into a thief—he has only gone back to his old safe-cracking ways to help the young girl. Others might think he has changed back because of the ease with which he slipped back into safe-cracking mode.

C Literary Focus

Possible answer: Ben pretends not to know Jimmy because he saw Jimmy do a good deed and show he is a changed man who does not need to go to prison anymore.

D Read and Discuss

To appreciate the ironic ending—Ben Price had been on Jimmy's trail for a very long time and now that he had the opportunity to arrest him, he let him walk away: **How did things turn out for Jimmy?** Possible response: Pretty good. After Jimmy saw Ben, he assumed Ben would arrest him, but instead Ben told him he didn't know who he was and referred to him as Mr. Spencer.

Comprehension Wrap-Up
Possible responses:
1. Ben Price saw that Jimmy was a changed man.
2. He fell in love with Annabel and wanted to be an honest man so that he could be with her.

Page 55
Applying Your Skills

Literary Focus
1. He wanted to get out of prison.
2. He wanted to steal money from safes.
3. He wanted to get to know Annabel.

Reading Focus
Possible answer: Ben is after Jimmy; Jimmy is avoiding Ben. They both see the good in Jimmy's changing.

Vocabulary Review
Possible answer: A Recovered Change.

THE WISE OLD WOMAN *AND* MRS. FLOWERS

Major Understanding for Read and Discuss Queries: This story tells a tale of a village where a ruler feels the elderly are useless and should be sent away to die. Eventually, one elderly woman saves the ruler's village and changes his opinion of the elderly and their place in society.

Page 57
A Read and Discuss

To set up the story's conflict—there is a cruel ruler who has decided that elderly people are useless. Because of this belief, once the villagers turn 71, they are banished to the mountains: **What has the author told us so far?** Possible response: There is a mean ruler who feels the elderly are useless, so as soon as they turn 71, he sends them off to the mountains to die. **Follow-up: What do the villagers think of this new law?** Possible response: They think it is dreadful, but they are so afraid of him, they won't disobey him.

Page 58
A Read and Discuss

To establish that one of the women in the village has turned 71 and must go to the mountains, but her son can't bring himself to broach the issue: **What is going on with this mother and son?** Possible response: The mother has turned 71 and must now go to the mountains to die, but her son can't bring himself to take her. The mother finally tells her son she knows it's her time.

C Read and Discuss

To draw attention to the farmer's solution—he digs a hole in the kitchen floor where he hides

Holt Adapted Reader Answer Key

his mother: **What is the son's plan to save his mother?** Possible response: He has decided to hide his mother, so he digs a hole in the kitchen floor where she will live.

D Read and Discuss
To understand the town's new problem—a neighboring lord is going to conquer the village unless someone is able to produce a rope of ash: **What is happening in the village now?** Possible response: The lord of a nearby town is threatening to conquer the village unless they can produce a rope of ash.

Page 59
E Read and Discuss
What do the villagers think of the proposal by Lord Higa? Possible response: They think it is impossible to make a rope made of ash and have resigned themselves to falling victim to another cruel lord.

Page 60
A Reading Focus
He is comparing the wise men to the young farmer's mother.

B Read and Discuss
To recognize that the farmer's mother was able to come up with a solution, allowing her son to make the ash rope and save the village: **How have things changed since Lord Higa first made his demand?** Possible response: The farmer's mother was able to figure out a way to make a rope of ash. Her son produced the rope and saved the village from the evil lord, winning the praises of the village's lord.

C Read and Discuss
To reinforce the pattern that has now developed—again the mother solved the problem: **Now what is going on with the evil lord? How does this new situation connect to Lord Higa's first demand?** Possible response: He's given the villagers another difficult task, and once again the farmer's mother was able to come up with a solution.

D Read and Discuss
How does this new situation connect to Lord Higa's first demand? Possible response: The farmer's mother once again solves the problem.

Page 61
F Literary Focus

Possible answer: The elderly are wise and should be respected and honored.

G Read and Discuss
To establish that the farmer finally admitted that it was his mother who was giving him the solutions to the lord's problems and to appreciate the lord's surprising reaction to that admission: **How do things turn out for the farmer and his mother?** Possible response: He finally admits that the solutions came from his mother, whom he had been hiding in his kitchen floor. Much to his surprise, the lord isn't angry; in fact, it helps him realize that the elderly are not useless. Rather, they should be respected for the wisdom of their years. **Follow-up: How do things turn out for the ruler and the villagers?** Possible response: Because he learns the error of his ways, the lord allows all people, elderly included, to live in the village peacefully, and it becomes a much better place.

Comprehension Wrap-Up
1. Possible response: Older people have much wisdom from their many years of living.

Page 62

Major Understanding for Read and Discuss Queries: Mrs. Flowers literally gave the mute Maya her voice back as the woman created a turning point in young Maya's life.

A Language Coach
biscuit

Page 63
D Read and Discuss
To develop the understanding that Mrs. Flowers drew out the silent Maya/Marguerite through her praise and attention, but likewise challenged her to read aloud the books that she'd share with the child: **What is Mrs. Flowers up to?** Possible response: Mrs. Flowers talks convincingly with Marguerite alone praising her written work, and encouraging her to consider what she is missing. She shares books with the child but Marguerite must read them aloud. Mrs. Flowers' plan is to get Marguerite to speak. **Follow-up: What does Marguerite think when Mrs. Flowers says, "Words need a person's voice to fill them with meaning"?** Possible response: Maya/Marguerite takes

Holt Adapted Reader Answer Key

Mrs. Flowers' words to heart, memorizing them because they seem so true and poetic.

E Read and Discuss
To assess the meaning behind the seemingly insignificant childhood details Maya recalls and explains with great precision: **What is the author saying with all of this?** Possible response: Maya/Marguerite goes to Mrs. Flowers' house and has cookies and lemonade, but the detailed description from a long-ago childhood indicates powerful, significant memories of this grand lady who takes time with Maya/Marguerite.

F Reading Focus
Possible answer: She is no longer hanging around alone feeling unhappy and unwanted.

Page 64
A Read and Discuss
To emphasize that Mrs. Flowers was a force of nature who instructed, coached, and insisted on Maya's/Marguerite's follow-through: **What has the author learned from Mrs. Flowers? What, in turn, is the author teaching us?** Possible response: Mrs. Flowers models expressive reading for the enthralled Marguerite, then, slyly insists that the girl visit again with a poem to recite. In addition to getting Maya to speak, Mrs. Flowers instructs the girl in "lessons in living" as she calls them—and who better to give these lessons than the perfect Mrs. Flowers!

B Reading Focus
Possible answer: They both enjoy reading and understand the importance of being respected.

C Read and Discuss
To acknowledge the benefit of Mrs. Flowers' strong presence in Maya/Marguerite's young life: **What is Maya Angelou's message?** Possible response: Uppermost in Maya's mind was that Mrs. Flowers liked her for just who she was and treated her in a special way. Mrs. Flowers seemed to fulfill Maya's deep need at the time.

D Reading Focus
Possible answer: Both Marguerite and the son in "The Wise Old Woman" have the opportunity to learn from the experience of older people around them. Both come to place greater value on the wisdom gained through experience by their elders.

Page 65
Applying Your Skills
Comprehension Wrap-Up
1. Possible response: Mrs. Flowers helps Marguerite speak up, learn life lessons, and realize she is special. Marguerite is fascinated by her.

Literary Focus
Possible answers:
1. Folk tales are designed to teach lessons. Characters in these tales are not real but rather represent traits or characteristics being discussed. An autobiography tells the author's life story. The characters in this type of book are real people.
2. Both the folk tale and the autobiographical passage tell a story from start to end using a combination of narrative and dialogue.

Reading Focus
1. Possible answer: The farmer's mother and Mrs. Flowers acted alike in that they helped others and knew the importance of doing so. They also advised the younger people in their lives—the mother, her son; Mrs. Flowers, Marguerite. The mother and Mrs. Flowers were both kind and wise.

Vocabulary Review
1. impressed   2. recite

PREAMBLE TO THE CONSTITUTION

Major Understanding for Read and Discuss Queries: The Preamble of the Constitution sets up what will follow and tells the reader what to expect in the document—that it will detail our rights, liberties and the structure of our government.

Page 67
B Read and Discuss
To establish that the Preamble lays out what will follow in the Constitution: **What does the Preamble tell us?** Possible response: The Preamble sets up what will follow in the Constitution—that it will detail our rights and the structure of our government as the crafters of the document wanted it to be.

Comprehension Wrap-Up
1. Possible response: It provides an overview of the objectives of the framers of the

Holt Adapted Reader Answer Key

Constitution, which will be spelled out in the document.

BILL OF RIGHTS

Major Understanding for Read and Discuss Queries: This article shows us the dramatic power of the Bill of Rights, that it was conceived centuries before, and that its (and the Constitution's) crafters understood that the Constitution would need to be changed and molded as time carried on and Americans shaped their lives in this new country.

Page 68
A Read and Discuss
To establish that Americans weren't fully satisfied with the Constitution as it was originally written—they added components to it to further protect the interests of Americans: **What has the author given us here?** Possible response: The author has shown us that Americans were worried that the Constitution didn't go far enough in protecting their rights—they added to it (made amendments) to ensure that it did. **Follow-up: Why do you think the writers of the Constitution included a way to change it?** Possible response: The people who wrote it knew it wasn't perfect and wanted to be sure it could be altered to ensure the citizens of America believed in it.

Page 70
A Reading Focus
They talk about people's rights within the legal system. They spell out what the people and their government can, cannot, and must do.

C Reading Focus
Possible answers: "serious"/ "straightforward"/ "clear"

Comprehension Wrap-Up
1. Possible response: We see court cases in the news every day. This is an example of the Bill of Rights in action, as everyone is entitled to a speedy, public, and fair trial.

DON'T KNOW MUCH ABOUT LIBERTY

Major Understanding for Read and Discuss Queries: This article demonstrates the frightening lack of knowledge Americans have about the freedoms they make use of every single day.

Page 71
C Read and Discuss
To set up that recent research demonstrated Americans are not serious about knowing their history and the freedoms that were ensured by the work of our forefathers, but Americans are well versed in pop-culture silliness: **What does it tell us about Americans that they know more about a TV show than about the First Amendment?** Possible response: Americans are not learning important matters of our history, but they are schooled in the lives of cartoon characters.

Page 72
A Reading Focus
Possible answers: "funny," "playful"

B Reading Focus
Possible answer: Yes, it makes the information easier to understand because the headings spell out the freedoms, and then the text below tells why those freedoms were sought.

Page 73
C Vocabulary
Minority means "the smaller number of something."

D Read and Discuss
To solidify the idea that the freedoms were designed carefully and as a result of having to live in the restrictive way the colonists did under British rule: **What does the information about why each amendment was created tell us about life before they were written?** Possible response: It sounds like life was very different for the colonists before they had the freedoms. The founders didn't just dream up ideas that sounded good, they saw the need to have these freedoms written in black and white so that no one could ever take them away.

Page 74
Skills Practice
Use a Compare and Contrast Chart
Students' charts will vary, but should reflect an understanding of treatment, scope, and organization in the three documents.

Holt Adapted Reader Answer Key

Page 75
Applying Your Skills
Comprehension Wrap-Up
1. Possible responses: We see newspapers and news shows on television reporting freely. Sometimes we see unions picketing during a strike.

Informational Text Focus
1. A   2. B
3. A   4. C

Vocabulary Review
1. preamble   2. liberty
3. majority   4. minority

SKILLS REVIEW

Page 76
Vocabulary Review
1. burglar   2. warden
3. liberty   4. amendments
5. constitution

Underline:
1. "gave the correct answer"
2. "liked to dress well"
3. "practice"
4. "no one's life, liberty, or property can be taken away without a trial"
5. "from his suitcase"
6. "influence"

Page 77
Language Coach
1. c   2. e
3. a   4. b
5. d

Oral Language Activity
Students' answers will vary, but students should come up with dialogue that is appropriate for the characters they choose.

Collection 3

THE MEDICINE BAG

Major Understanding for Read and Discuss Queries: *A young man, Martin, of Sioux Indian heritage learns that there are ways to* incorporate his grandpa's traditions into the modern world in which Martin lives. The story explores what it means to live in one community while living with one's history and traditions—traditions that may conflict with but also contribute to who someone is inside and out.

Page 81
B Read and Discuss
To establish that the narrator and his sister Cheryl use exaggerated tales of their Grandpa and their experiences on the Sioux Indian reservation to garner attention—that they're embarrassed that their Grandpa's real image doesn't fit the TV version of Indians: **What do you know about the lives of the narrator and his sister?** Possible response: They entertain their city friends with tales from their vacations at their Grandpa's home on the Sioux reservation. **Follow-up: Why does the narrator tell his friends about his grandfather but never show them his picture?** Possible response: The narrator is afraid his friends would be disappointed, because Grandpa doesn't look like a TV Indian.

Page 82
A Read and Discuss
To begin to explore the narrator's complex feelings toward Grandpa: **What does Martin's reaction to Grandpa's arrival tell you about his attitude towards Grandpa?** Possible response: His reaction shows that although he's incredibly self-conscious about his Grandpa, he is protective of him, too.

B Read and Discuss
To further develop the narrator's mixed emotions at seeing his Grandpa: **How does the narrator's attitude towards Grandpa's clothing add to what you know about his thoughts towards Grandpa?** Possible response: This scene shows again that the narrator is embarrassed by his Grandpa's appearance—yet when he looks into his Grandpa's face he sees weariness and protectively helps lead him up the driveway.

Page 83
D Read and Discuss
To discern that Grandpa is ill and that Martin respects Grandpa's traditions and expectations: **What has happened?** Possible Response: Grandpa is sick and everyone is

taking care of him. **Follow-up: What do Martin's actions toward Grandpa show us about the way Martin feels for him and Sioux traditions?** Possible response: Martin's actions show he understands and respects Grandpa's expectations and traditions that govern the way people dress, act,—that Grandpa wouldn't want to be undressed by his granddaughter—and show affection.

E Read and Discuss
To establish the shift in Martin's view of the way Grandpa made his "embarrassing" arrival: **What does Martin think of Grandpa now?** Possible response: After hearing Grandpa's tale of why and how he arrived at Martin's home, Martin is proud of Grandpa—no trace of the shame he felt earlier.

F Vocabulary
Circle: (c)

Page 84
A Read and Discuss
To call attention to another shift in Martin's thoughts and feelings: **What is the medicine bag?** Possible Response: It is a treasure passed down through generations—it's Martin's turn to have it, but he's not so sure he wants it. **Follow-up: How does the passing of the medicine bag connect to Grandfather saying "Do not feel bad that you didn't bring me with you I would not have come then."** Possible response: Grandpa is saying he had to wait to make the journey until he was ready to give the medicine bag to Martin—that only when Grandpa realized he was going to die was he ready to go to Martin's home. **Follow-up: Why does Martin have mixed feelings about taking the medicine bag?** Possible response: Martin imagines wearing it everywhere he goes, having his friends make fun of him. He's not comfortable expressing his heritage that way, but knows he must take it.

B Literary Focus
Possible answer: Grandpa's actions connect to the theme of concern about appearances.

Page 85
C Read and Discuss
To establish that Martin is learning he had nothing to fear in introducing his friends to Grandpa: **What is Martin learning from Grandpa's visit?** Possible response: Martin

sees that Grandpa will try not to embarrass him, and that his friends are enthralled by Grandpa to the point of politeness.

D Reading Focus
Possible answer: The slow beat of the drum in Martin's dream may relate to the thoughts he is having about his American Indian culture. Dreams may reflect the activity of the subconscious.

E Read and Discuss
To highlight the great respect Martin has for Grandpa and the way he does things, even though he doesn't yet understand what's happening: **Why do you think Martin enters Grandpa's room and just sits there in dark, not doing anything until Grandpa addresses him?** Possible Response: Again Martin shows that he is respectful of Grandpa even though he's not sure he wants to be part of the medicine bag ritual and has no idea what's involved in the process.

Page 86
A Literary Focus
Possible answer: The name comes from the wise old men of the tribe to whom Grandpa's father told his dream. It refers to the piece of iron he found and believed protected him.

B Read and Discuss
To recognize that Grandpa and his ancestors believed the medicine bag provided protection and held clues to future endeavors during extremely difficult times: **What does Grandpa's retelling of the history of the medicine bag tell us about his people?** Possible response: Grandpa and his ancestors believe the medicine bag protected and in veiled ways portended what their lives were to entail in the future—they have faith that spirits will guide each man with the bag. **Follow-up: How does Grandpa think the bag connects to the death of Martin's grandfather?** Possible response: Grandpa seems to think that if Martin's mother's father had taken his bag to the war, he might not have died there.

C Reading Focus
Possible answer: Sioux society has very defined roles. Men are considered stronger mentally and emotionally, as Grandpa says the things he tells Martin are only for men's ears, and that is why he sent his daughter and Cheryl away while he told his story. It is not

Holt Adapted Reader Answer Key

proper for his daughter to hear it, Grandpa says.

Page 87
D Read and Discuss
To establish that Grandpa is far more wise than Martin gave him credit for: **Based on what we know about Martin, what will he think of Grandpa's orders not to wear the bag on a daily basis?** Possible response: He'll realize his Grandpa is wise and that he understands Martin's life far better than Martin understood Grandpa's.

E Read and Discuss
To discern that Martin is on the reservation, finding sage for his bag because Grandpa died: **What does Martin putting the holy plant in his medicine bag let us know about Grandpa?** Possible response: Grandpa died and now Martin has the opportunity to add the holy plant (precious sage) to his medicine bag.

Comprehension Wrap-Up
1. Possible response: Martine will likely hold the bag dearly, because he respects and admires Grandpa and Sioux traditions.

Page 88
Skills Practice
Use a Concept Map
Possible answers:
1. Martin: Self-conscious of Grandpa around other kids, respectful of Grandpa's traditions
2. Grandpa: Traditional, kind, understanding, wise, teller of great stories
3. Other Characters: Martin's mom and Cheryl love when Grandpa visits, they are not self-conscious like Martin
4. Theme: Respecting tradition; not placing a great deal of importance on what others think

Page 89
Applying Your Skills
Literary Focus
1. Martin
2. Possible answers: Respecting and honoring tradition, not caring about appearances or what others think, growing up, rites of passage.

Reading Focus
Circle: 1, 3, 4, and 6

Vocabulary Review
1. vision   2. reservation
3. Sioux

A SHOT AT IT

Major Understanding for Read and Discuss Queries: "A Shot at It" is a true story of the author's push to improve herself and her situation so that she can leave the crowded Brooklyn community she detests. With the help of interested teachers, Esmeralda Santiago eventually graduates from the Performing Arts High School and Harvard.

Page 91
A Read and Discuss
To establish that Esmeralda is new to the school and is meeting with the counselor to discuss her future: **How is the author starting things off?** Possible response: The author has started at a new school in a new country. She finds speaking English difficult, but reads and writes at a tenth-grade level despite being in ninth grade. **Follow-up: What does Esmeralda's conversation with the counselor uncover?** Possible response: The counselor tells Esmeralda that her test results indicate that she is suited for nursing and teaching careers because she likes helping others. Esmeralda doesn't find those choices appealing.

Page 92
B Read and Discuss
To recognize that when the counselor presses for an answer to what Esmeralda plans to do with her life, she gives an answer without thinking: **What is happening in Mr. Barone's office?** Possible response: When Esmeralda offhandedly responds that she wants to be on television, Mr. Barone, the counselor, decides on an audition for the Performing Arts High School for her.

Page 93
C Literary Focus
Possible answer: Esmeralda wants a shot at college because she wants to get out of Brooklyn, where her family has settled.

D Read and Discuss
To highlight that Esmeralda now has a focus because of the audition and that there is hope that she can leave the hated Brooklyn: **What**

is on Esmeralda's mind? Possible response: The author hates her crowded, frightening neighborhood and sees the audition as a way out.

Page 94
A Reading Focus
Possible answer: When first asked that question by Mr. Barone, Esmeralda did not have any plans or hopes for the future. Now, Esmeralda knows what she wants and will do whatever it takes to get it. The connection is in having goals and pursuing them no matter what happens.

B Literary Focus
Possible answer: What Mr. Barone means is that Esmeralda has a chance at getting into the school. This point connects to the theme of working hard to achieve your goals and having hopes.

C Read and Discuss
To acknowledge that many will help Esmeralda to prepare for the Performing Arts High School audition: **How does Mami help Esmeralda prepare for her audition?** Mami buys her daughter suitable clothing that the teachers suggested and allows Esmeralda to wear some makeup. **Follow-up: How does Mami seem to feel about the School for the Performing Arts?** Although Mami seems proud and hopeful for her daughter, the school is far from their home.

Page 95
D Read and Discuss
To highlight the tension of Esmeralda's audition and her feelings about its outcome: **What happened in the audition?** Possible response: The three imposing women on the audition panel made Esmeralda so nervous that she forgot the calm, confident way she was supposed to behave. She raced through her speech, jumbling all the words together and even tossing in Spanish words. Esmeralda was certain, because of all her blunders, that she would never be accepted.

Page 96
A Literary Focus
Possible answer: Esmeralda's audition shows that you can be yourself and draw from your own experience. Moreover, you don't have to forget where you came from just because you want to change your current situation in life.

B Read and Discuss
To set up the story's surprises conveyed through the epilogue – Esmeralda was accepted at the Performing Arts High School, graduated and went to Harvard on a scholarship, and one panel member became her mentor: **What is the author letting us know in the section titled "One of These Days"?** Possible response: Esmeralda must have been a bright, dedicated student to be accepted at the Performing Arts High School and at Harvard on a scholarship, as well. **Follow-up: What story does the teacher reminisce about?** Possible response: Because Esmeralda didn't have proper clothes to wear and because she had to go with Mother to translate for her, Esmeralda couldn't go to the first day of class. The teacher called, heard the explanation, and Esmeralda was able to begin the next day.

Page 97
Comprehension Wrap-Up
1. Possible response: Yes, if you try hard, you can make changes for the better and achieve your goals.

HOW I LEARNED ENGLISH

Major Understanding for Read and Discuss Queries: "How I Learned English" is a humorous snapshot of the way one poet began his journey toward becoming "one of the boys." In a broader sense, he discovers that learning English goes beyond the words a person speaks.

Page 98
A Read and Discuss
To set up the narrator's unease with his place in America and in the baseball game, and to begin to establish his lighthearted nature: **What is happening in this scene?** Possible response: The narrator, who is new to America, is describing the boys he is playing baseball with and his own discomfort in not knowing how to play. **Follow-up: The narrator uses words like "wiffed" to describe his experience playing baseball. What do light and playful words like this tell us about the narrator?** Possible response: Although the narrator is describing a difficult situation in his life, his words are light—maybe indicating he has a sense of humor about it.

Holt Adapted Reader Answer Key

Page 99

B Literary Focus

Possible answers: A theme in this poem is coming to a new country and learning how to get along and speak the language. "A Shot At It" also covered the author's difficulties in immigrating, learning a new language, and trying to progress.

C Read and Discuss

Why are the boys laughing? Possible response: The boys are laughing because the narrator has referred to the wrong body part when describing his injury. This makes his misfortune more difficult to take seriously.

Page 100

A Read and Discuss

To elicit that in being able to laugh at himself, the author endeared himself to his new friends: **Why does the author say that his laughing and Joe's helping him up were so important?** Possible response: It seems as though the narrator is saying that because he was able to laugh at himself along with the others, a situation was created that brought them together as friends for the first time.

B Read and Discuss

What kind of boy is the narrator? Possible response: He's introspective, but not so serious that he misses the humor hidden in what could be embarrassing situations.

Comprehension Wrap-Up

1. Possible response: Being the new kid is not easy. On top of that, it would be hard to laugh at yourself in an embarrassing situation with new people who all know each other, but it would be a good thing to do. By laughing at yourself, you show you do not take yourself too seriously and that you can have a sense of humor about things. This happened with the narrator, and it seemed to help him make friends.

ED MCMAHON IS IRANIAN

Major Understanding for Read and Discuss Queries: This short story deals with a young Iranian-American girl and her family during the time that 52 Americans were held hostage in Iran and the retribution that resulted against this family. Dad's joke relieved the young child's mind at the time and the extension of his joke continued to amuse the family years later. A humorous remark can surely ease the sting of a wrong done.

Page 102

A Read and Discuss

To establish that the Iranian-born family was targeted for punishment while Father eases his daughter's tension over the situation with a simple explanation: **What has happened?** Possible response: The five-year-old narrator tries to make sense of the paint thrown at the family's door and asks Dad for an answer. He tells her someone did it because they are mad at the Iranians who are holding 52 Americans as prisoners. The girl is confused, saying she and her family didn't do anything. Her father tells her that she is correct but that the people who threw the paint think it is their fault.

B Reading Focus

Possible answer: Each reading has to do with getting along in a new country, trying to find one's place, and trying to be happy there.

C Read and Discuss

To determine that dad's joke about Iranians moved the family beyond the tension of the attack: **What effect does Father's joke have on Mariam?** Possible response: The five year old is feeling isolated, wishing to be simply American and says, "No one here is Iranian." Father quickly points to Ed McMahon on TV saying that he is Iranian. Every time Ed's face shows up on TV or in the mail, the girl feels better and the family, too, enjoys the joke. **Follow-up: Why do you think she enjoys the joke years later, even though she knows it is a trick?** Mariam can laugh now because she can appreciate that she was just a child trying to fit in, and because it is all in the past.

Comprehension Wrap-Up

1. Possible response: Father tells Mariam that Ed McMahon is Iranian so that she will feel better by thinking that there are Iranians—famous ones, at that—in America.

Page 103

Applying Your Skills

Literary Focus

1. A Shot At It; autobiography of a Puerto Rican girl who moves to Brooklyn and is helped by her guidance counselor.

Holt Adapted Reader Answer Key

2. account of an immigrant boy's first baseball game; memoir.
3. Ed McMahon is Iranian; essay.

Reading Focus

Possible answer: The common theme is moving somewhere new and facing hardships while still achieving what you want—whether that is to be an actress, to make new friends playing baseball, or to learn of and appreciate others who are in your situation (Ed McMahon being an "Iranian" in America, for instance).

Vocabulary Review

Students' answers will vary, but should demonstrate a clear understanding of the word that provides the focus of each exercise.

LEWIS AND CLARK: INTO THE UNKNOWN

Major Understanding for Read and Discuss Queries: Students should understand that President Jefferson purchased a large amount of land, the Louisiana Purchase, and then recruited Meriwether Lewis to lead an expedition across that land, hoping to discover the Northwest Passage. Although the Northwest Passage was never discovered, the journey was still worthwhile.

Page 105
A Read and Discuss

To establish that the United States had just purchased a piece of land known as the Louisiana Purchase and that the president, Thomas Jefferson, wanted explorers to cross that new land and possibly find the Northwest Passage – a water route to the Pacific: **What did President Thomas Jefferson do that changed the country?** Possible response: The United States just bought some land called the Louisiana Purchase, and President Thomas Jefferson wanted explorers to cross that land and see what they could find.

Page 106
B Read and Discuss

To recognize that President Jefferson was pulling together a group of explorers to prepare for the journey across the Louisiana Purchase: **Why was the Corps of Discovery formed?** Possible response: President Jefferson had to select people for the trip

across the land. Specifically, he selected a man named Meriwether Lewis to lead the expedition. **Follow-up: What was the big deal about being chosen as leader?** Possible response: Because the territory was unknown, Lewis had to be trained in many areas – navigation, zoology, botany, and medicine. He then selected a co-leader and together they selected and trained four-dozen men to be members of their "Corps of Discovery." In other words, being leader was quite a job!

C Reading Focus

Possible answers: Cause: Lewis and Clark knew they could not cross the land without help from Native Americans. Effects: The expedition party was welcomed by many tribes, but had problems with others.

Page 107
D Read and Discuss

To set up the problem the explorers faced and their solution to that problem – they needed horses to cross the mountains and Sacagawea helped them procure the horses: **What problem did Lewis and Clark have?** Possible response: They needed horses to cross the mountains, and they needed to get these horses from the Native Americans, so they needed some to help with the negotiations. **Follow-up:** *To establish the role the Native American woman Sacagawea played in Lewis and Clark's journey:* **How did Sacagawea help Lewis and Clark?** Possible response: A Native American woman named Sacagawea helped with the negotiations with various tribes so that the corps was able to buy horses and acquire other aid they needed.

E Read and Discuss

To discern that although the journey was treacherous and the explorers never did find the Northwest Passage, it was still a worthwhile effort: **How did things turn out for the explorers when their trip was done?** Possible response: It was a really rough journey with wild animals and treacherous rapids, and unfortunately, they never did find the Northwest Passage. However, it was still a worthwhile journey, as they identified many unknown landmarks, plants, and animals.

Comprehension Wrap-Up
1. Possible response: They must have been brave, intelligent, curious, and determined.

Holt Adapted Reader Answer Key

Page 108
Skills Practice
Use a Cause-and-Effect Map
Possible answers:
Causes:
   2. The group needs horses.
   3. The group encounters hardships.
Effects:
   1. The exploration leads to meetings with tribes and new discoveries of plants and animals.
   2. They hire Sacagawea and her husband, who translate and help in other ways.
   3. They do not find the Northwest Passage.

Page 109
Applying Your Skills
Literary Focus
   1. B   **2.** C

Vocabulary Review
Possible answers:
   1. connoisseurs, masters, those with special or superior skills or knowledge in a particular area
   2. group, unit, company, division, body, service, organization, band

LEWIS AND CLARK REVISITED

Major Understanding for Read and Discuss Queries: Students should understand the term "reenactment" and be able to describe the differences between this particular historical reenactment and the original journey taken by Lewis and Clark.

Page 111
B Read and Discuss
To establish that a group of people were going to recreate the Lewis and Clark expedition:
What has the author told us about the Discovery Expedition? Possible response: It was an expedition on which about 177 people reenacted the Lewis and Clark expedition.
Follow-up: How did the two journeys differ? The first expedition was practical—Lewis and Clark were exploring the new territory. The second expedition was symbolic and educational.

Page 112
B Reading Focus

Possible answer: Lewis and Clark had to rely on food they found en route, including animals they hunted, while those in the reenactment could eat modern food provided by visitors.

C Vocabulary
Threatened means "endangered."

Page 113
E Read and Discuss
To reinforce how the two expeditions differed:
What other things do we learn about the two journeys? Possible response: Again, the two expeditions differed greatly. Lewis and Clark relied on the Native Americans to help them along their journey, while the re-enactors had just a little of that experience. Lewis and Clark faced the dangers of the unknown, including wildlife, while the re-enactors faced far less danger.

Page 114
A Reading Focus
Possible answer: Both groups achieved their main goals and helped people to learn new things.

B Reading Focus
The author used the point-by-point method.

C Reading Focus
Possible answer: The author wants to show how much things have changed since the original trip.

Comprehension Wrap-Up
   1. Possible responses: People are interested in the journey and want to see how times have changed. They could learn these things firsthand by going on such an adventure, and feel connected to an important part of history.

Page 115
Applying Your Skills
Informational Text Focus
Possible answers:
   1. Corps of Discovery: Over 200 years ago; peace-making and trade mission; more animals and plants along the way; tools and medicines of their time; covered selves in animal fat to fight mosquitoes; boats with oars, poles, sails, and ropes; first winter camp in Camp Wood, Illinois.
   2. Discovery Expedition: Modern; educational mission; fewer animals and

   Holt Adapted Reader Answer Key

plants along the way; some supplies similar to the originals; camp placed two miles away form original location because Mississippi River has moved east since first trip; video meetings; pizza and donuts.

3. Both: Were welcome with some Native American tribes and not welcome with others.

Vocabulary Review
1. expedition; reenactment
2. satellite

SKILLS REVIEW

Page 116
Vocabulary Review
1. Sioux
2. transfixed
3. expert
4. satellite
5. convey

Students' sentences will vary, but should reflect an understanding of the vocabulary words.

Page 117
Language Coach
Circle: "corps"

Writing Activity
Possible answer: The main theme behind each of the stories is coming to a new country and finding happiness, whether it is through accomplishing a goal, fitting in, or finding others like you. Esmeralda in "A Shot At It" faces the conflict of getting through her audition; the boy in "How I Learned English" deals with saying the wrong word during a baseball game and being laughed at; and the girl in "Ed McMahon is Iranian" wants to be American and does not believe there are any Iranians in America. All of them find ways to overcome their problems. The main idea that connects each story is that one can find a way to get through hardships and tough scenarios.

Collection 4

THE TELL-TALE HEART

Major Understanding for Read and Discuss Queries: Students should understand the narrator's question of madness versus wisdom and appreciate the author's language and detail concerning the narrator's crime and eventual breakdown.

Page 121
A Read and Discuss
To set the stage and introduce the idea of someone being nervous, mad, or having overly acute senses: **This paragraph is a bit confusing. What have we learned so far?** Possible response: The narrator seems to be struggling with the idea that he is either mad or has really sharp senses. In either event, he appears to be rather nervous about something.

Page 122
B Read and Discuss
To set up the suspense that the narrator might get caught: **How are things looking for the narrator now?** Possible response: Not good. As he is looking in the room, his finger slips and makes a noise, causing the old man to sit up and ask, "Who's there?"

C Reading Focus
Possible answer: When I finally had the chance, I shined the light on the old man's eye.

D Literary Focus
It is ironic that the narrator feels terrified too because he is the one who is responsible for the violence.

Page 123
F Vocabulary
A *corpse* is a dead body; Circle: "body".

G Read and Discuss
To address the gory details of the cover-up of the crime and the fact that the narrator is quite proud of his deed: **The narrator gives a vivid description of how he handled the body and the crime scene. What point is he trying to make?** Possible response: He is quite proud of how he dismembered the body, used a tub to catch the blood, and then hid the body underneath the floor planks. **Follow-up: How does this information connect to our previous discussions about the narrator?** Possible response: He is nuts!

Holt Adapted Reader Answer Key

Page 124
C Literary Focus
Possible answer: No, the police officers didn't hear the heart, because it beat only in the narrator's imagination. What is ironic is that the narrator did a good job of hiding the body, but his guilt, mixed with insanity, led him to reveal that he was the killer.

D Read and Discuss
To highlight that the "noise" of the beating heart led the narrator to tear up the planks and expose the hideous crime: **How did things turn out for the narrator?** Possible response: Not good. While he was talking to the police, he was convinced he could hear the old man's heart beating louder and louder, until he could no longer take the noise. As a result, he pulled up the planks and exposed the corpse.

Comprehension Wrap-Up
Possible responses:
1. It is clear from the narrator's actions and the descriptions of his thoughts that he is mad.
2. The old man's beating heart represents the guilt the narrator felt for the crime he committed.
3. Poe provides a window into the insane world of the narrator through his choice of words and the details he provides in the story.

Page 125
Applying Your Skills
Literary Focus
Possible answers:
1. The narrator says the officers are making a "cruel joke" of his horror, but he is the one responsible for the horror of murder.
2. It appears at first that the narrator's skill in hiding the body and his calm manner will throw off the police. But his guilt and insanity lead him to be caught.
3. The narrator thinks his mental state has improved his senses, but the reader knows that the narrator's insanity on display.

Reading Focus
1. Possible answer: You think I'm crazy? Think about what a good job I did of hiding the corpse.
2. Possible answer: I couldn't stand it anymore. I had to do something. The heart keeps getting louder.

Vocabulary Review
1. corpse   2. chatted
3. shrieked

RAYMOND'S RUN

Major Understanding for Read and Discuss Queries: "Raymond's Run" presents a powerful, though in the end, flexible character who isn't afraid to work toward a goal. The story demonstrates the goodness in Squeaky and the way she works with her life constraints to be the type of person she wants to be—important.

Page 128
A Read and Discuss
To discern that being the best runner in town defines who Squeaky is for herself: **Why does Squeaky talk about running so much?** Possible response: Running seems to define who Squeaky is—it's the thing that makes her feel good about herself.

B Literary Focus
Underline "ain't"; They are walking up Broadway and the street is not that wide.

D Read and Discuss
To further develop Squeaky's defensiveness and solitary nature: **How does this scene with the three girls add to what we know about Squeaky?** Possible response: The scene shows that Squeaky is always thinking, anticipating others' actions and taking a strong stand against anything she sees as insulting to her or Raymond. **Follow-up: How do Squeaky's thoughts that girls don't know how to smile at each other connect to her solitary nature?** Possible response: Aside from having to care for her brother and training for her races, Squeaky doesn't seem to trust anyone and isn't inclined to be friends with other girls.

E Reading Focus
Possible answer: Squeaky and Raymond have a loving and caring relationship.

Page 129
F Read and Discuss
To further establish Squeaky's cheeky view of the world: **How does Squeaky's description of the May Pole dancing add to our image of her?** Possible response: All of this is

further indication of her dry sense of humor and the staunch way she knows what's important and has no time for anything frivolous.

G Vocabulary
Here, *break* means "opportunity."

Page 130
B Read and Discuss
To discern that it's not clear whether Squeaky won the race and to consider how Squeaky might handle a loss: **What's happening with Squeaky, Gretchen, and the race results?** Possible response: It's not clear who won the race because it was so close. **Follow-up: Knowing what we do about Squeaky and her attitude toward running, how might she handle a loss?** Possible response: Squeaky is so driven and intense that she probably won't accept a loss very well. It might feel like she's losing a part of her identity if she isn't known as the fastest runner in town.

D Reading Focus
Possible answer: Squeaky is reexamining her priorities. She is thinking more about how she can help her less fortunate brother Raymond.

Page 131
Applying Your Skills
Literary Focus
Possible answers:
1. "[Rosie] says a lot of mean things about Raymond. But the two of them are similar. She is not in a position to judge."
2. "You are correct. If anyone says anything else, they will be in trouble with me."

Reading Focus
Students' paragraphs will vary, but should reflect an understanding of the details that make up the story.

Vocabulary Review
1. fly   2. break
3. chicken

FROM RAY BRADBURY IS ON FIRE!

Major Understanding for Read and Discuss Queries: Through this interview, we meet the prolific science fiction writer Ray Bradbury and find that he is critical of the computer, the car, and in general, those electronic devices that diminish human interactions.

Page 133
A Read and Discuss
To establish Ray Bradbury's viewpoint—keep it real, keep it human: **What strikes you as interesting in this description of Ray Bradbury?** Possible response: Because Bradbury is often categorized as a science fiction writer, we might assume that he's enthusiastic about new inventions. However, he's actually skeptical about devices that lessen human contact and interactions. **Follow-up: What is paramount for Ray Bradbury?** Possible response: Bradbury says no electronic shortcuts nor distracting entertainment can replace human contact and active thinking, so human engagement is key for him.

Page 134
B Read and Discuss
To have the students discern Mr. Bradbury's manner of writing—he writes daily using a typewriter or pen and draws his ideas from personal creativity and from a rich background of myths: **What is Bradbury saying about his manner of working?** Possible response: He loves writing. He has a background in myths from many cultures and seems at no loss for ideas, cranking out short stories daily. **Follow-up: What's this about Bradbury's computer?** Possible response: He's probably saying the typewriter or writing by hand would be more immediate, more real. He says he has no need of a computer.

C Reading Focus
Possible answer: Bradbury believes that people who do not read cannot think effectively.

D Read and Discuss
To recognize why the author sees worth in reading: **What is the value of reading for Bradbury?** Possible response: He says, "If you can't read and write you can't think." He feels that without recording one's thoughts, the ideas vanish, and there can be no introspection.

Comprehension Wrap-Up
Possible responses:
1. It is difficult to categorize Bradbury. He is a complex person and writer who makes us rethink the labels we use.

2. Reading is necessary for a civilization to function properly. Reading is also a requirement of being able to think well.

THE FLYING MACHINE

Major Understanding for Read and Discuss Queries: *In this dark fairy tale, an Emperor maintains the balance in his land (everyone is "neither too happy nor too sad") by controlling what his people can encounter. To that extreme, he must execute a man with a tremendous invention that could possibly upset the balance of the land.*

Page 135
A Read and Discuss
To set up the background: An Emperor is quite content with the way his land is run—the people are not too happy, not too sad. Suddenly a servant brings him some fascinating news: **What has the author told us about this Emperor and his people?** Possible response: Emperor Yuan rules land near the Great Wall of China and is content with the way things are going. The people are "okay" – they are "not too happy or too sad." **Follow-up: What's this about a miracle?** Possible response: A servant tells the Emperor he has seen a man flying.

B Vocabulary
Possible answer: *Bamboo* must be lightweight and flexible—suitable for making wings like a bird's.

Page 136
A Reading Focus
Possible answer: He mistakenly thinks the Emperor will greet his invention with enthusiasm; Underline: "came proudly".

B Read and Discuss
To recognize that the Emperor doesn't seem to like the idea of the flying man: **What does the conversation between the Emperor and the flying man tell us about the Emperor's thoughts?** Possible response: He doesn't seem to be impressed with the idea that the man made a machine that enabled him to fly. In fact, he questions the man to make sure no one else knows of his invention.

C Literary Focus

Possible answer: Author Ray Bradbury and his character Emperor Yuan share a fear of and distaste for technological advancements.

Page 137
D Read and Discuss
To establish that the man is trying to convince the Emperor that his flying machine is as beautiful as the Emperor's own invention: **What is the flying man up to now?** Possible response: He's trying to plead his case to the Emperor. When the Emperor shows him his invention of a mechanical garden and tells him how beautiful it is, the man tries to convince the Emperor that his flying machine is every bit as beautiful.

Page 138
A Read and Discuss
To reinforce the reason for the execution: **What do you think the Emperor means when he says, "What is the life of one man against those of a million others?"** Possible response: The Emperor believes in order to maintain balance in his land, he must keep this invention a secret. The only way to ensure that the invention stays a secret is to execute the inventor. He feels justified in taking one life to maintain the balance in so many others' lives.

B Literary Focus
Possible answer: By setting the story in ancient China, Bradbury is saying that the wrong technology can be dangerous anywhere.

Comprehension Wrap-Up
Possible responses:
1. Perhaps he feels that the inventor is more dangerous. If the inventor lived, he could create more dangerous devices.
2. The two inventions are a pair of wings that enable a man to fly and a three-dimensional landscape with moving metal parts. The Emperor believes that only his invention (the second one) is beautiful because it provides enjoyment but cannot harm anyone.

THE DRAGON

Major Understanding for Read and Discuss Queries: *In "The Dragon", Bradbury begins to weave one story thread and by the end, the reader finds an entirely different thread is part* *of the tapestry. Two knights believe they're about to battle a legendary dragon, but when they're no match for the fierce "monster" the story reveals two train employees who believe they've hit a knight (ghosts?) who wouldn't leave the train tracks.*

Page 139
B Literary Focus
Possible answers to underline: "I loved dinosaurs from the age of five"/ "I met and became friends with Ray Harryhausen"/ "we loved airplanes, rocket ships, trolley cars, and trains."

Page 140
A Vocabulary
Possible answer: The dragon is very violent with his victims.

B Read and Discuss
To set up that two knights are discussing a legendary dragon and their chances in slaying it after so many have tried and failed: **What has the author set up for us with the knights' conversation?** Possible response: Two knights are discussing the power of a dragon who repeatedly slays people in the same spot. One knight seems afraid to take his chances in killing it.

Page 141
C Reading Focus
Armor is something that might protect the knights against the dragon.

D Read and Discuss
What information has the author given us in these first four panels? Possible response: These panels give a sense of the fear that the dragon causes, and that the struggle against it has gone on for a long time.

E Vocabulary
Possible answer: Familiar words that start with *trans-* include "transportation", "transact", and "transcend". These words all convey a sense of crossing. So, *in transit* appears to mean "traveling" or "going across".

Page 142
A Vocabulary
Possible answer: Girded in armor, the knights point their lances in the dragon's direction and charge toward it.

B Reading Focus
Possible answer: It seems likely that the dragon will attack the knights head-on. Circle: "rounded"/ "flung".

C Read and Discuss
How do the illustrations help build suspense? Possible response: The illustrations show the fear on the faces of the knights and the fierceness of the dragon as the knights perceive him.

Page 143
D Read and Discuss
To establish that both knights and their horses were killed by the great dragon: **What has happened to the knights?** Possible response: Both knights were easily killed by the mighty dragon.

Page 144
A Read and Discuss
To recognize that there seem to be two stories going on at once—both with characters passing through the same space at the same time but belonging to different eras. **How do the train engineers figure into a story about knights and a mighty dragon?** Possible response: The train is what the knights think of as the dragon, and that explains why they can't kill it. **Follow-up: How does the text "The wind was a thousand souls dying and all time confused and in transit. It was fog inside of a mist inside of a darkness" connect to the events of the story?** Possible response: The sentences try to explain, perhaps, why two sets of people living centuries apart have intersecting lives. It's something metaphysical and mysterious.

Page 145
Applying Your Skills
Comprehension Wrap-Up
Possible responses:
1. Describing the dragon, the story states: "His eyes are fire, his breath a white gas." These correspond to the train's lights and its smoke and steam, respectively.
2. The author creates a convincing and frightening story by setting a tone, providing details that support the tone, and drawing parallels over time.

Literary Focus
Possible answer: Bradbury believes that certain technology can be dangerous. His

Holt Adapted Reader Answer Key

writing reflects this stance in illustrating both positive and negative aspects of technology.

Reading Focus
Possible answers:
1. In the interview, Bradbury says, "You've got to be able to look at your thoughts on paper and discover what a fool you were." He believes that the process of writing allows him to grow and better develop his thoughts.
2. The Emperor has the inventor of the flying machine executed because the inventor did not fully consider the ramifications of his contraption.

Vocabulary Review
Circle: sentence (2)

STEAM RISING: THE REVOLUTIONARY POWER OF PADDLEBOATS

Major Understanding for Read and Discuss Queries: The article highlights the need for and the lure of the paddlewheel steamboat. Also, it focuses on Robert Fulton and others who designed and modified such transports, which enabled swift movement of people and materials on the rivers in United States.

Page 147
B Read and Discuss
To establish reasons for current interest in paddlewheel boats: **What do we learn about modern-day travelers and the steamboat?** Possible response: Even though paddle steamboats are outdated, some people, eager for long-gone experiences, are interested in a slow, peaceful ride.

C Read and Discuss
To recognize the advantages of paddlewheel steamboats: **What was so special about the paddle steamboats?** Possible response: There were a lot of advantages to the paddlewheel steamboats: freight could travel faster than on earlier boats; the boats could sail in shallow water due to their flat-bottomed design; no time was wasted waiting for a windy day to sail as these boats were powered by steam.

Page 148

A Read and Discuss
To recognize the developing advances that led to Fulton's successful transport, the Clermont: **How does this information connect to what you read on the first page?** Possible response: Building on advancements in others' boat designs, Robert Fulton's Clermont, a paddlewheel steamboat, sailed inland at nearly 5 mph so that goods could be delivered more quickly than ever before without relying on the wind.

C Read and Discuss
To acknowledge that the paddlewheel steamboat is gaining popularity: **What is the point of these statistics?** Possible response: Improvements in engineering waterways and improvements to the paddleboat's design and safety raised the boat's popularity, productivity, and attraction.

SUMMARIES OF "STEAM RISING"

Major Understanding for Read and Discuss Queries: The two summaries—the first more concise than the second—give the main understandings of the companion text, "Steam Rising: The Revolutionary Power of Paddleboats".

Page 149
F Reading Focus
Possible answer: This summary does cover the article's main ideas and provide enough supporting details. Summary 2 summarizes the article's main ideas in roughly the same order they were presented, while Summary 1 reverses their order.

G Read and Discuss
To compare and contrast the two summaries: **What do these summaries show you?** Possible response: These two summaries illustrate two ways to summarize the text "Steam Rising." The second one is longer and more detailed in its retelling of the information about the paddle steamboat's design, its inventors, and the impact of this boat on American history. The second summary gives more detail through examples and statistics while the first summary is more concise in its explanations.

Holt Adapted Reader Answer Key

Page 150
Skills Practice
Use a Venn Diagram
Possible answers:

1. Summary 1: did not include the full title or the author's name. The summary stated the article's topic, but it did not report the main ideas in the order they appeared in the article. Summary 1 did provide some supporting details and one quotation from the article.

2. Both: The two summaries provide at least part of the article's title. Both also give the article's purpose and at least some main ideas and supporting details.

3. Summary 2: begins by stating the article's full title, author, and topic. It then summarizes the main ideas in the same order as they appeared in the article. Summary 2 supplies numerous supporting details but no quotations.

Page 151
Applying Your Skills
Comprehension Wrap-Up
Possible responses:

1. Even though trains travel faster than steamboats, steamboats are irreplaceable in the sense that they provide an enjoyable, nostalgic method of transportation.

2. Steamboats expanded trade, allowing our nation to grow and make better use of its resources.

Informational Text Focus
Students' summaries will vary. Here is one possible answer: Jessica Cohn's "Steam Rising: The Revolutionary Power of Paddleboats" reviews the creation, development, and impact of the steamboat in America. Inventors began attempting to create a new form of transportation in the late eighteenth century, but the first working steamboat was not built until 1802 by Robert Fulton. Fulton was well educated and his steamboat served America's growing trade and transportation needs. Steamboats continued to evolve into the nineteenth century and are still being used today.

Vocabulary Review
1. twinkling   2. method   3. upriver

Page 152
Vocabulary Review
Circle:

1. whispered   2. forever
3. ignored   4. chicken
5. confusion   6. untie
7. shrug   8. chair
9. crawl   10. corpse
11. ordinary

Page 153
Language Coach
Students' answers will vary, but should reflect an understanding of the multiple meanings of each word.

Oral Language Activity
Students' answers will vary, but students should use evidence from the texts to support their answers in their conversations.

Collection 5

FROM HARRIET TUBMAN: CONDUCTOR ON THE UNDERGROUND RAILROAD

Major Understanding for Read and Discuss Queries: This excerpt highlights an especially difficult trip on the Underground Railroad. It shows Harriet Tubman's intelligence in handling, encouraging, and prodding fellow slaves to freedom even when they become discouraged and begin to think slavery is better than the difficult trip.

Page 158
A Read and Discuss
To set up that a man named Moses is using secret signals to help slaves run away: **What has the author set up for us?** Possible response: A man named Moses sneaks into slave quarters and helps slaves escape. He uses different animal calls to signal he's arrived. **Follow up: What does this use of animal signals tell us about Moses?** Possible response: He is smart; using signals that are

only slightly different from the way they'd be heard in nature.

Page 159
C Read and Discuss
To discern that the man known as Moses is actually Harriet Tubman: **What have we learned about Moses now?** Possible response: The man that the slave masters think of as "Moses" is actually Harriet Tubman.

D Reading Focus
Possible answer: Tubman's goal is to help more and more slaves make their way toward freedom. This could be the main idea, because this is the reason Tubman plans and conducts their escapes.

Page 160
A Read and Discuss
To recognize that the Fugitive Slave Law made escaping much more difficult and dangerous: **Why does the author name several escaped slaves in talking about the Fugitive Slave Law?** Possible response: It sounds like at one time, the law was only loosely enforced, but now, people Harriet knew were being re-captured and sent back home to face their former masters. **Follow up: How did the enforcement of this law impact Harriet?** Possible Response: Not only was it more dangerous for her to help take slaves to freedom because of what could happen if she were caught, but she also had to take the slaves all the way to Canada to find freedom.

B Literary Focus
Possible answers: Underline: "She had never been to Canada"/ "But she could not let the runaways who accompanied her know this"

Page 161
C Vocabulary
Incentive means "something to stimulate or encourage greater action"; Harriet knew that if she spoke of the promise of warmth and good food, it would encourage the runaways to keep going along on their difficult journey.

E Read and Discuss
To understand the tenuous nature of the Underground Railroad: **What is happening with Harriet and her group?** Possible response: They're being turned away from the first stop on the Underground Railroad.

Follow Up: What does this turn of events show you about the trip they are taking? Possible response: This incident shows how fragile the Underground Railroad was—that it went from having reliable stops to being completely unavailable to Harriet and those that she brought with her.

Page 162
A Read and Discuss
To recognize how intelligent Harriet was to manage to keep the slaves moving through disappointment and physical hardship: **How did Harriet manage to keep her group going even when they were tired, afraid or not scared enough?** Possible response: Harriet had to constantly monitor their emotional and physical status to be able to give them the right kind of encouragement and help them keep going all the time. **Follow up: What does this show us about Harriet Tubman?** She was incredibly perceptive, smart and determined to bring her group to freedom. She understood when to calm her group, when to fill them with hopeful stories, and when to prod them with the knowledge that their hunters weren't far behind.

Page 163
D Literary Focus
Possible answer: Because she hesitated, we know Harriet Tubman was not sure whether she would see friend of foe on the other side of the door. The fact that Harriet Tubman stopped and said a prayer in a time of need shows us that she has a firm belief in God. She was a woman with a tremendous amount of faith and courage, who was hopeful that after all of their tiresome travels and hardships, this stop on the Underground Railroad would provide some safety and shelter for the group.

Page 164
A Read and Discuss
To establish that finally Harriet and her group found some relief: **What is going on now?** Possible response: Harriet and her group finally got a good night's sleep at a stop on the Underground Railroad.

Page 165
C Reading Focus
Possible answer: This story is connected to the main idea because it illustrates the extremes

Holt Adapted Reader Answer Key

people had to go to in order to pave their way to freedom and to help others find freedom.

D Language Coach
Eloquence means "speaking in a way that illustrates an artful use of language"

Page 166
A Read and Discuss
To recognize that the toll of the trip is showing itself in the attitudes of the slaves and that Harriet will let nothing stand in their way of freedom: **What is going on between Harriet and her group?** Possible response: Harriet is trying to instill hope in her weary, tired group, but they aren't interested in her stories of other slaves or the people who helped them. **How does Harriet carrying a gun connect to what we know about her?** Possible response: Harriet seems to be gentle and compassionate, but she has clearly learned she might need a gun to ensure the success of their trip.

Page 167
C Vocabulary
Indomitable means "cannot be subdued or overcome; unconquerable"; Possible answer: This shows that Harriet Tubman looked strong, like someone who would not be beaten.

D Read and Discuss
To discern that Harriet has completely convinced her group that freedom or death in pursuit of Freedom is their only option: **How does the gun fit into the story now?** Possible Response: The idea that Harriet falls asleep and her gun is available to her group, yet no one uses it and they don't take advantage of Harriet's sleeping to leave, shows she has thoroughly convinced the group they must carry on to freedom.

E Literary Focus
Possible answer: Every aspect of Tubman's personality comes together on this page, as she is a strong and determined leader, a fearless defender of rights, and a staunch advocate of freedom. Tubman vows that she will either get these people to freedom like she promised, or she will die trying—which shows her dedication to these people.

Page 168
A Read and Discuss

To highlight the incredible gift in William Still's risky undertaking of writing down fugitive slaves' histories: **How can we describe William Still's record keeping of the slaves who used the Underground Railroad?** Possible response: It was both risky and wonderful. Risky because if anyone had found the records before slavery ended they all could have faced criminal charges, but wonderful because it is a gift to be able to understand the trials and tribulations that individual slaves underwent to claim the freedom that should have been theirs all along.

Page 169
C Vocabulary
Fastidious means "hard to please."

D Read and Discuss
To establish that Harriet and her group finally made it to Canada: **What has happened by the end of the selection?** Possible response: Harriet and her group of eleven slaves finally made it to Canada after a month.

Comprehension Wrap-Up
Possible responses:
1. Harriet Tubman was a strong and determined leader—a fearless defender of human rights, and a staunch advocate for freedom. She had faith, she was compassionate, and she was tough.
2. The runaways' trip from Maryland to Canada had many ups and downs, because it was a long journey and they were often tired, hungry, and without shelter. They also constantly feared getting caught.
3. The name "Moses" was biblically a man's name. Also, Harriet wore a disguise, and people at that time may not have even been able to imagine that a woman could be so sneaky and so strong.

Page 170
Skills Practice
Use a Time Line
Possible answers:
1. Tubman and her group of runaways made stops on the Underground Railroad, trying to get food and shelter for one night at a time.
2. The group gets turned away from a house that had provided shelter for Harriet before.
3. The group finally reached another stop on the Underground Railroad, and were taken

Holt Adapted Reader Answer Key

into a warm house and given food and rest for the night.

4. It took them a month, but the group finally made it to freedom in Canada with the help of several others along the way.

Page 171
Applying Your Skills
Literary Focus
Possible answers:

1. Harriet Tubman went to the farm to collect eleven runaway slaves and begin her journey to Canada. She made animal noises and sang songs about Moses to signal to them that she had arrived.
2. Harriet knew just when to encourage the group by telling them wonderful stories about freedom and promising them warm shelter, food, and a good nights rest soon.
3. One man threatened to leave the group and return to slavery in Maryland when the trip got difficult, and Harriet said she would shoot him if he left, because they would make him reveal how the Underground Railroad worked upon his return.
4. With help from kind people, the group finally made it to Canada, after a month, and were free.

Reading Focus
Possible answers:
Important detail: Harriet Tubman led slaves to freedom by way of the Underground Railroad.
Important detail: The Fugitive Slave Law made it much more dangerous to help runaways, but Tubman vowed to get them to freedom or die trying.
Important detail: Some people along the way would take the group in for the night and feed and shelter them so that they could continue on their journey.
Main Idea: Harriet Tubman was a brave woman who guided many slaves to freedom.

Vocabulary Review:
1. Circle: "fled from"
2. Circle: "could not understand"
3. Circle: "wonderful speech with confidence."

FRAGMENT ON SLAVERY, 1854

Major Understanding for Read and Discuss Queries: This piece written by Abraham

Lincoln debunks what has been at times offered as logical reasoning for taking and retaining black people as slaves.

Page 173
B Reading Focus
Possible answers: Circle: "By this rule you will become a slave to the first man you meet who has lighter skin than you."/ "And if it helps his life, then he has the right to make you his slave."

C Read and Discuss
To weed through the logic Lincoln put forth to debunk some arguments in support of slavery:
What is Lincoln doing with all these examples? Possible response: Lincoln is using simple logic to discredit several arguments that hold that it is appropriate and reasonable for white people to enslave black people.

Comprehension Wrap-Up
1. Possible response: Lincoln's argument and logic still make sense in today's world. There could always be someone who is fairer or smarter than another, but those are certainly not justifications to enslave another person.

WHAT TO THE SLAVE IS THE FOURTH OF JULY?

Major Understanding for Read and Discuss Queries: In this excerpt from Frederick Douglass's speech, the students should understand that Douglass is trying to evoke enough passion from his listeners to prompt them to take quick action against slavery. He recognizes that a simple speech wouldn't have the same impact and tries to spark their emotions with a vivid description of the realities of slavery.

Page 174
B Reading Focus
Underline: "'American Slavery'"

Page 175
D Reading Focus
Possible answer: Slaves are humans, too, just as their owners are.

F Read and Discuss

To address that Douglass has finally made it clear as to why he isn't going to argue against slavery – something bigger than an argument is needed in order to get rid of slavery: **It now becomes clearer why Douglass kept saying that he was not going to argue certain things. What does he say is needed more than just arguments?** Possible response: Douglass believed it would take more than a convincing argument to rid the country of slavery. He felt it would take a movement as big as an earthquake to make a change in a country and its views concerning slavery—and he felt that change was a necessity.

Comprehension Wrap-Up:

1. Possible response: Douglass's speech shows just how terrible and wrong he thinks slavery is. It also shows that Douglass feels the country needs to change right away, and should not wait a minute longer.

Page 176
Skills Practice
Use a Concept Map
Possible answers:
Proposition: There is no logical argument one can make to justify the enslavement of others.
Support:
1. Fairer skin color does not justify slavery.
2. Greater intelligence does not justify slavery.
3. Personal convenience does not justify slavery.

Page 177
Applying Your Skills
Informational Text Focus
1. d   2. b
3. d

Vocabulary Review
Possible answer: Liberty is any person's state of being free. A person cannot truly be free, however, if he or she is a slave.

SKILLS REVIEW

Page 178
Vocabulary Review
1. dispel   2. define
3. fugitives   4. prove

5. issue   6. reactions
7. incentive   8. liberty

Students' answers will vary, as they must make up the rest of the story about how Marc tries to get a man to overcome his prejudice against teenagers. Possible answer: Marc met a man who had a prejudice, or bias, against teenagers. To persuade him that not all teenagers are bad, Marc took the man to a soup kitchen where he volunteers with many other teenagers.

Page 179
Language Coach
Students' answers will vary. Place the possible following answers in the correct boxes:
1. concede: *v.:* to acknowledge; to admit; to give in. Sentence: Even though he was losing in the polls, the presidential candidate refused to concede until all of the votes were counted.
2. precede: *v.:* to go or come before. Sentence: A standup comedian will precede the band's performance.
3. recede: *v.:* to retreat; to go away. Sentence: When the general saw that his army was greatly outnumbered, he gave the signal for his troops to recede into hiding.

Oral Language Activity
Students' answers will vary, but speeches are acceptable if they meet the given requirements: using one of the phrases given, and supporting the proposition with at least two of the following: facts, examples, definitions, expert opinions, or anecdotes.

Collection 6

SKATEBOARD PARK DOCUMENTS

Major Understanding for Read and Discuss Queries: This combination of texts presents students with data and opinions related to the installation of a skateboard park in a fictional town. Grappling with the information in the texts will allow students to form their own data-based opinion on whether the park is feasible.

Page 183
C Reading Focus
Circle: "2.1 acres in the 15-acre sports park at Ramp and Spin avenues."

D Read and Discuss
To establish that the memo presents facts that, so far, support the development of a skateboard park: **According to this information, why is there a need for a skateboard park?** Possible response: The information in the memo seems to indicate a solid group of people in town who would make good use of a skateboard park. **Follow-up: What does the information in the other sections of the memo tell us?** Possible response: The memo spotlights the ways having a skateboard park is doable—local groups have already raised half the money necessary—and having a park wouldn't add any liability to the city.

Page 184
A Reading Focus
Underline: "The City Beat."
Students should recognize that this is a public document from the title, byline, and nature of the article.

B Vocabulary
Possible answer: In the first paragraph, the word *risks* refers to potential harm that may come to the city. In the second paragraph, *risks* roughly means "chances." The meaning of *hazards* is closer to the first usage of *risks*.

Page 185
D Read and Discuss
To recognize that the article highlights varying opinions regarding skateboarders and the development of a park on the skateboarders' behalf: **How do all of the different citizen comments add to the debate?** Possible response: The citizens muddy the debate with their opinions. It's necessary to hear the opinions, but the facts in the memo are easier to characterize as a pro or con. *To discern that Mr. Owner's proposal will add to the viability of developing a skateboard park:* **Follow-up: How does the information Mr. Owner shares add to the argument?** Possible response: Mr. Owner's proposal to lower the cost of safety equipment is met with great support. His plan and the citizens' response to it, seems to add to the

sense that the skateboard project will go forward.

Page 186
A Reading Focus
Possible answer: This is a coupon that offers 50 percent off at the Skate Bowl. This is the discount that Mr. Owner promised to offer in the previous document about the debate.

B Reading Focus
Possible answer: The small text is important because it discusses the specifics of the discount. For instance, it lists items at the Skate Bowl for which the discount does not apply. It is important for customers to read the small text so they know what to expect.

Page 187
D Reading Focus
Possible answer: In "The City Beat" article, many people said that skateboarders need smooth and safe places to skate. This excerpt supports that by saying that many accidents happen because of hazards like bad riding surfaces. This document also cites injury statistics, which supports the need for the safety equipment that Mr. Owners offered at a discounted rate.

Page 188
Skills Practice
Use a Venn Diagram
Possible answers:
1. Skateboard Park: These documents present information to help the residents of a town to decide whether or not they should build a skateboard park.
2. Same: In both sets of documents, attention to detail is important. For instance, potential customers at the Skate Bowl must read the small print on the coupon to ensure that they fully understand the offer. Similarly, Juan must read the SweetPlayer user's agreement carefully.
3. SweetPlayer: These documents are intended to help individuals decide if they should purchase the SweetPlayer.

Page 189
Applying Your Skills
Comprehension Wrap-Up
1. Possible response: The information in the first document contains research and mostly discusses the issues facing the

Holt Adapted Reader Answer Key

parks department. It generally supports the skate park by telling about its benefits. The second document presents public information. It contains opinions both for and against the park. The excerpt is also a public document for consumers. It contains research and facts about skateboarding accidents and safety. In general, that document supports the idea of having a safe park.

Informational Text Focus
Students should place checkmarks in the following boxes under the specified headings:
1. Critical Issues Memorandum—check the 2nd, 3rd, and 5th boxes down under the heading.
2. The City Beat Column—check the 1st, 3rd, 4th, 5th, and 6th boxes down under the heading.
3. Excerpt from Consumer Product Safety Commission: Document 93—check the 1st, 3rd, and 5th boxes down under the heading.

Reading Focus
Possible answer: After previewing SweetPlayer documents, I think that I will learn about downloading music from the Internet.

Vocabulary Review
Students' sentences will vary, but must correctly and logically use two of these three words: *potentially*, *proposal*, and *hazards*.

SWEETPLAYER DOCUMENTS

Major Understanding for Read and Discuss Queries: This informational piece describes an advertisement for SweetPlayer, software that enables music to be downloaded from the Internet. The article stresses the user agreement that describes the legality of downloading and using music.

Page 191
C Vocabulary
Students should recognize that a Web site's *copyright* will indicate if it is legal to copy material from that site.

D Read and Discuss
To understand what music one can legally download and use from the Internet: **What**
does this box say about downloading music?** Possible response: If the Internet music is for you alone, you can download promo tracks that are free, or you can buy music tracks that are for sale. **Follow up: What other information is given?** Possible response: You can copy a CD to your computer as long as the music is for your own use.

Page 192
A Reading Focus
Possible answer: We don't know how much SweetPlayer costs. We know that the Deluxe version costs $19.95 for a limited time. Without knowing how much the basic version costs, it is

B Read and Discuss
To discern the difference between SweetPlayer and SweetPlayer Deluxe: **What do we learn in this box about SweetPlayer?** Possible response: The SweetPlayer offers easy downloads, Web radio stations, and good sound quality. **Follow up: What is the author telling us about the SweetPlayer Deluxe?** Possible response: With the deluxe version, it seems that you get more features.

Page 193
C Reading Focus
Possible answer: The step-by-step directions and descriptions of actions for the user to perform are common elements of technical directions.

Page 194
C Reading Focus
Possible answer: It would be a poor decision to skim or scan a user's agreement because you might miss important information about your responsibilities as a user.

Page 195
D Reading Focus
Possible answer: Circle: "SweetPlayer, Inc., guarantees that the software will work for sixty (60) days"/ "SweetPlayer, Inc., may…replace defective media, advise you on how to achieve described performance, or refund the license-agreement fee."

E Read and Discuss
To acknowledge the significance of the user's agreement and its time limits: **When Juan accepts the user's agreement, what does**

Holt Adapted Reader Answer Key

that mean? Possible response: The license means Juan can use the software for himself only, he agrees to follow the copyright laws, SweetPlayer owns the rights to this software, and the person uses but doesn't own it, and cannot sell it to anyone else. **Follow up: What other information is important for Juan to understand?** Possible response: For 60 days the software will do what's needed if Juan follows the directions. If there's a software problem, the company will decide on the measures to be taken.

Page 196
Skills Practice

Use a Skimming and Scanning Chart
Possible answers:
What I learned from skimming:
1. Juan is examining the legality of downloading music from the Internet.
2. Juan is considering the SweetPlayer software for listening to music on his family's computer.
3. Juan has decided to download the SweetPlayer Deluxe. He is doing following the directions to do so.
4. Juan plans to accept the software user's agreement, which specifies rules Juan must follow if he buys SweetPlayer.
5. The SweetPlayer warrantee is good for 60 days. If your software is damaged, the company that makes SweetPlayer has the final say in what steps may be taken.

What I learned from scanning:
6. This page discusses MP3 players and when downloading music from the Internet is legal.
7. The company that makes SweetPlayer also offers a Deluxe model, which seems to have more features.
8. There are seven steps for downloading SweetPlayer Deluxe, each with specific instructions.
9. There are several conditions in the SweetPlayer software user's agreement that describe how the software may be used legally. This page shows four of those conditions.
10. This is the Limited Warrantee page, which costumers should read thoroughly.

Page 197
Applying Your Skills
Comprehension Wrap-Up

Possible responses:
1. Users may only download music for their personal use. Sharing music is usually illegal. Most music downloaded from the Internet must be paid for, unless it is specifically marked "free."
2. If a person clicks "Accept" without reading a contract, he or she could miss important information about the user's responsibilities. If a person does not know his or her responsibilities as a user, he or she might unknowingly break the law.

Informational Text Focus
Circle: "directions for downloading"/ "license agreement"/ "ad for 30-day trial"/ "60-day guarantee that software will work"
Underline: "one-click downloading"/ "software can be used on any two computers"

Reading Focus
Students' answers for questions 1 and 2 will vary, but should illustrate that students properly skimmed the "Guide to Computers." Scan question, possible answer: Connect the monitor and printer to the computer, connect the mouse and keyboard, and finally connect the modem and power cords.

Vocabulary Review
Possible answer: Juan agrees to *abide* by the terms and conditions, or rules, of using the SweetPlayer software.

GUIDE TO COMPUTERS

Major Understanding for Read and Discuss Queries: This is an exercise in reading technical directions in order to set up a computer.

Page 199
B Read and Discuss
To understand the importance of following technical directions so that one can operate electronic devices properly: **What point is the author trying to make here?** Possible response: When you want to operate mechanical or scientific devices, technical directions will tell you how to do that. **Follow-up: What is the strict definition of a computer and how does that connect to technical directions?** Possible response: A computer is any "electronic device that performs tasks by processing and storing

information." So in order to perform a task, the manual will probably need to be consulted so that the input can be properly stored and processed to ensure the expected output.

Page 200
A Reading Focus
Possible answer: The boxes show the functions, or uses, of a computer and the arrows show the order in which the functions are performed.

B Vocabulary
Possible answer: *Processes* is just a different form of the verb *processing*. When a computer *processes*, it works to examine information.

Page 201
C Reading Focus
Possible answer: This portion of the directions is a parts list. It is important because it is necessary to have all of the correct parts in order to assemble a computer.

D Language Coach
Possible answer: Here, *handles* roughly means "manages" or "deals with."

Page 202
A Read and Discuss
To focus on the idea that each part of the computer's hardware relates to a separate chore (function) to be handled: **What does this part say about the computer's hardware?** Possible response: Each part of the computer has a specific task that it performs. For example, to enter information into the computer, the keyboard is used. Each piece of hardware is separate, but the parts and functions are interrelated and depend on each other.

Page 203
D Read and Discuss
To understand the purpose of the Internet and how the global network operates: **What is the purpose of the Internet?** Possible response: The Internet network enables many users to share information. **Follow-up: How is this done?** Possible response: Connecting a multitude of computers allows computer users to "talk" to one another. Phone lines in users' homes connect to ISPs (Internet service providers) that connect, in turn, to satellites. The information then is returned to the computers through the ISPs and the phone lines.

Page 204
A Reading Focus
Possible answer: One diagram shows a larger area of the CPU, while the other shows a close-up of the CPU. The first diagram helps a reader understand all the parts of the CPU and the close-up shows how to connect a cable to one part of the CPU.

Page 205
C Read and Discuss
To demonstrate the benefits of having both a diagram and sequential directions in order to set up one's computer: **Why would a diagram and text both be included in the directions?** Possible response: The written text explains the order in which to follow the directions while the diagram can show a particular segment in a clearer way. The diagram is a visual description while the text can give more details. Some people prefer to work from a diagram, others from text.

Page 206
Skills Practice
Use a Graphics Table
Students' graphics illustrations will vary, but should provide a logical visual aid to accompany each step in the "Technical Directions" column.

Page 207
Applying Your Skills
Comprehension Wrap-Up
Possible responses:
1. A clock may be a computer if it is digital and has a computer inside. Also, you input information into a clock and the clock outputs information. For example, when you set an alarm on a clock, you are inputting the time when you want the clock alarm to sound. The clock processes the information and stores it until the time you set. It outputs the alarm sound at the time you input. You might need to consult technical directions for a clock to learn how to set the time and the alarm.
2. The parts and functions of a computer include: input devices like a keyboard or mouse; the central processing unit (CPU) which collects and processes input; the memory, which stores input; the output

Holt Adapted Reader Answer Key

devices, like monitors and printers, which display the information; and modems, which allow computers to talk to each other and exchange information. It is important to understand the parts and functions of an electronic device so you can assemble and operate it.

Informational Text Focus
Possible answers:
1. One can look at the graphic in Step 4 of the technical directions.
2. One can find this information in the Computer Hardware section, or parts list, under the heading "Memory."
3. One can double-check the steps in the technical directions section, which is titled "How to Set Up a Desktop Computer."

Reading Focus
Students' graphic illustrations will vary, but should logically illustrate one step in setting up a computer.

Vocabulary Review
1. corresponding
2. functions

SKILLS REVIEW

Page 208
Vocabulary Review
Students' sample sentences will vary, but should demonstrate an understanding of each vocabulary word. Students' definitions may also vary slightly.
1. potentially (puh TEHN shuh lee) *adv.:* possibly.
2. abide (uh BYD) *v.:* to remain, continue, or stay.
3. sequence (SEE kwehns) *n.:* order.
4. functions (FUHNGK shuhnz) *n.:* uses or jobs that something performs.
5. proposal (pruh POH zuhl) *n.:* suggestion.
6. fundamental (fuhn duh MEHN tuhl) *adj.:* basic; essential.

Page 209
Language Coach
Circle:
1. "il" in illegal
2. "un" in uncover
3. "re" in rewrite
4. "un" in unfashionable

5. "im" in impossible
6. "semi" in semicircle
7. "extra" in extraordinary
8. "dis" in disconnected

Students should identify that any two of the three prefixes *il-*, *un-*, and *im-* all roughly mean "not" or "no." For instance, *illegal* means "not legal," as *impossible* means "not possible."

Writing Activity
Students' answers will vary. Possible answer: There are many documents I would read before buying a new MP3 player. I would read advertisements to compare the costs and features of different players. I might also read newspaper articles that compare the different MP3 players and discuss their features. I would also read the warranties to see what promises the company makes about taking care of the product. Finally, I would also read the user's agreements, in case there is anything that I have to do as the customer.

Collection 7

VALENTINE FOR ERNEST MANN

Major Understanding for Read and Discuss Queries: This fun poem asks the reader to look at the world differently as the poet illustrates how to find poetry in unexpected places.

Page 213
A Read and Discuss
To establish that the poet believes poetry resides everywhere in life if we only take the time to find it: **What has the poet set up for us?** Possible response: The poet offers a tale of a person who "orders" a poem. **Follow up: What does the way the poet replied to the letter show us about her view of writing poetry?** Possible Response: She seems to find it amusing that someone ordered a poem, but clearly believes if the person just looks closer at his life, he'd find his own poem. Even under his foot, or somewhere not ordinarily associated with poetry.

B Reading Focus

Holt Adapted Reader Answer Key

Possible answer: Reading the poem aloud gives it more personality. For instance, when I said the line: "In the bottoms of our shoes," it sounded more humorous, because it seems funny to suggest that poems are hiding in our shoes.

Page 214
B Reading Focus
Students' answers will vary but they should take note of and look up definitions for any words that are confusing.

C Read and Discuss
To recognize that even things normally seen as ugly can be viewed as beautiful poetry if you look at them in a different way: **How does the skunk story connect to the way the poet views the starting point and growth of poetry?** Possible response: The skunk story demonstrates that people who look beyond what they're expected to think can find truly unique poetry in everyday life—even in the eyes of ugly, smelly skunks.

Comprehension Wrap-Up
Possible responses:
1. Students should mention objects that otherwise seem ugly or repulsive to most people, such as insects, mud, Brussels sprouts, or certain kinds of music or art.
2. You would have to look for the good or beautiful things in the person you "almost like." All people have something special about them. It might be a physical feature, like their eyes, or a skill, like their ability at a sport or other activity.

Page 215
Applying Your Skills
Literary Focus
Possible answer: "Valentine for Ernest Mann" fits the definition of a lyric poem because it expresses the speaker's thoughts on poetry and perspective. The poem also conveys various feelings to the reader.
Possible details:
1. The speaker directly states her view on poetry when she says, "poems hide."
2. The speaker expresses her feelings about Valentine's Day when she shares the humorous story about the skunks.
3. The poem hints at strong emotion; I felt inspired upon completing it.

Reading Focus

Possible answers:
1. Read to enjoy: The first lines about ordering a poem like ordering a taco were funny. These lines showed that the poet had a sense of humor about writing poetry.
2. Read aloud: Reading this poem aloud can help a reader enjoy the poet's descriptions of where poems hide. Reading aloud can also help a reader hear the rhythm of the poem.
3. Knowing the meaning of *re-invent* can help a reader better understand the last lines of the poem. The poet is saying that we could find poetry if we remake things that are ugly, beautiful in our minds. This way, we can find a poem in almost anything.

Vocabulary Review
Students' sentences will vary. Possible answers:
1. The balloon was drifting in the breeze.
2. The little boy had a lot of spirit while he was playing on the playground.

PAUL REVERE'S RIDE

Major Understanding for Read and Discuss Queries: In his day, Henry Wadsworth Longfellow was a poet and story-teller extraordinaire who shaped the political thinking of the average American and developed the importance of our country and its collective stories. Although this poem is a detailed account of Paul Revere's ride to alert the citizens about the advancing British soldiers, the poem also created a national myth that is well worth telling and retelling.

Page 217
C Read and Discuss
To establish that there's a plan in place to warn citizens about the British soldiers, so that those in harm's way can prepare: **What is the speaker setting up?** Possible response: In April 1775, before the American Revolution began, Paul Revere had a plan to warn people if they were soon to be in danger. **Follow up: How will the plan work?** Possible response: Revere and his friend have worked out a system with signals. His friend will hang a lantern in the church steeple – one lantern if the British soldiers are coming to attack by land, and two lanterns if they are

Holt Adapted Reader Answer Key

coming to attack by the sea. Once the message is given, Revere will spread the word to the colonists so they can get better prepared.

Page 218
B Literary Focus
Possible answer: A fast rhythm, because it is a suspenseful part of the poem and each line leads directly into the next.

C Read and Discuss
To elicit that the British soldiers are moving toward their boats and Revere's cohort in the steeple tower understands this: **What is the speaker letting us know?** Possible response: The friend in the church tower listens, watches, and finally hears that the British soldiers are moving to the shore.

Page 219
D Reading Focus
Possible answer: Revere's friend snuck up to the church tower to look upon the town.

E Literary Focus
Possible answer: This poem just shows one narrator's point of view of the bigger picture: the British invasion that led to the start of the American Revolution.

Page 220
A Literary Focus
Possible answer: The rhythm of these lines is slow because in this part of the poem, Revere is looking up at the church tower and slowly realizing that there are now two lamps hanging in the tower. But because Revere comes upon this realization gradually, we must read these lines at a slower pace to match the mood of this particular part of the poem.

B Vocabulary
Circle: "A second lamp in the belfry"

C Read and Discuss
To discern that the two lamps in the belfry indicate that the British soldiers are indeed coming in boats: **So what has happened?** Possible response: Revere nervously awaits his cue. Finally, two lanterns hang as a signal for him to alert the people that the British are coming by way of the sea.

Page 221
D Language Coach

Light means "something which illuminates or affords visibility," and also, "something that is not heavy." Here, *light* means "something which illuminates or affords visibility."

E Reading Focus
Possible answer: All you could hear was the sound of the horse's hoofs hurrying down the village street, and all you could see was the dark figure of a man riding on horseback in the moonlight—but this was no ordinary man on a horse—this was Paul Revere riding for our nation's freedom.

Page 222
B Read and Discuss
To draw attention to Revere's night-long mission to communicate his message: **What is going on now?** Possible response: In the middle of the night, Revere gallops from village to village, notifying people of the British soldiers and their approach.

C Literary Focus
Possible answer: The conflict is that Paul Revere knows that once the British soldiers get on land, a bloody battle will ensue and many lives will be lost. He feels a bit helpless, because the only thing he can do is try to give fair warning. But he cannot save lives.

Page 223
E Read and Discuss
To set up that there is a shift in time so that in this part, the speaker is looking ahead to what will happen at Lexington and Concord when the colonists meet the British soldiers: **What is the poet describing here?** Possible response: In the village of Concord, the British soldiers meet the colonial farmers and there's fighting and death. We get a feeling of the farmers' bravery and persistence against the British. **Follow up: How does this connect to Revere's ride?** Possible response: Revere rides to warn the colonists, they prepare and meet the British soldiers in what came to be called the Battle of Lexington and Concord.

Page 224
A Vocabulary
Underline: "and not of fear"; The British want the colonists to fear them, but the colonists "refuse to obey," or, "defy" them.

B Read and Discuss

　Holt Adapted Reader Answer Key

To return to the story of Paul Revere's ride and its significance: **What is Longfellow trying to get across to the readers?** Possible response: Readers should feel the intensity and importance of Revere's mission to call the colonists to arm against the British. His ride is part of our U.S. history, and certainly, with Longfellow's telling, it "shall echo forevermore."

Comprehension Wrap-Up
Possible responses:
1. This poem serves as a narrative of an important event in the history of the United States.
2. The language in this poem is pretty complex, so it is unlikely that it is literally directed at young children. However, as citizens of the United States, we are all "children" of the American Revolution.

Page 225
Applying Your Skills
Literary Focus
Possible answers:
1. Paul Revere, his horse, his friend, the British and the colonists.
2. Massachusetts, April, 1775.
3. The British were coming to attack the colonies and Revere had to try to warn everyone so that they could be prepared to fight before it was too late.

Reading Focus
1. Possible answer: Paul Revere was impatient while he waited for the signal. He wanted there to be enough time for him to warn as many people as possible, so he was eager to get on his horse and ride.

Vocabulary Review
1. aghast   2. impetuous

ON THE GRASSHOPPER AND THE CRICKET

Major Understanding for Read and Discuss Queries: "On the Grasshopper and the Cricket" illustrates the beauty of a sliver of nature as Keats sees it, through the activities of grasshoppers and crickets.

Page 227

B Reading Focus
Possible answer: Keats illustrates the simple, though constant, ways that nature creates beautiful poetry, such as a grasshopper resting under a leaf while birds hide away from the heat. Keats shows that there is poetry present everywhere, if one just looks and listens closely enough to find it.

Page 228
B Read and Discuss
To establish that Keats sees poetry in the simple things in nature such as grasshoppers and crickets and that nature is forever changing–living: **How does the poem explain the line "The poetry of earth is never dead?"** Keats illustrates simple though constant ways nature creates beautiful poetry such as the grasshopper playing and resting under a leaf while birds hide away from the heat. Keats brings in different seasons to show there is poetry present and alive if one just looks—listens—close enough.

Comprehension Wrap-Up
1. Possible response: Keats seems to view nature as something to be celebrated at all times of the year. He finds wonder in the liveliness of the grasshopper throughout the heat of summer, and also in the cricket throughout the cold of winter. Keats seems to think that the world is full of things that should be celebrated in poetry.

Page 229
Applying Your Skills
Literary Focus
1. five   2. unstressed

Students' answers will vary, but students must correctly identify stressed and unstressed syllables in the line they choose.

Reading Focus
Possible answers:
1. The earth is always alive. The grasshopper is a good example, because it is happy during the heat of summer when even the birds hide.
2. The opening line.
3. In the last six lines, the cricket proves Keats' point again. In winter, the cricket comes alive and makes noise even when it is cold. Therefore, at every point in the year, there is always something alive about nature.

Vocabulary Review
1. b   2. a

SKILLS REVIEW

Page 230
Vocabulary

1. f	6. i
2. d	7. g
3. j	8. c
4. a	9. h
5. b	10. e

Page 231
Language Coach
Possible answers:
1. made with a lot of effort; hard to make
2. start from scratch and give something old an entirely new 'spin' to make it seem new.
3. to get someone to do or say something by 'egging them on.'

Oral Language Activity
Students' answers will vary, but students should reflect on how their interpretations of the poems compare and contrast when reading the poems aloud as opposed to hearing them read.

Collection 8

THE DIARY OF ANNE FRANK: ACT ONE, SCENES 1 AND 2

Major Understanding for Read and Discuss Queries: Anne Frank's diary, presented in play form, takes the reader from Anne's hiding place in an Amsterdam warehouse to the day, two years later, when the Nazi police remove the Frank family and their companions, transporting them to concentration camps. The impact of one teen's message to the world about her Holocaust captivity is a testament to the power of the written word.

Page 238
A Read and Discuss
To establish that following the end of World War II, Mr. Frank returns to thank Miep Gies for hiding his Jewish family. Miep gives Mr. Frank papers that had been left behind and he begins to read Anne's diary: **What is going on between Mr. Frank and Miep?** Possible response: Otto Frank, Anne's father, returns to the hiding place that had been his family's home for over two years. He returned to thank Miep Gies and Mr. Kraler who protected his Jewish family by helping them hide from the Nazis. Miep gives Mr. Frank papers that were left behind, including Anne's diary, and Mr. Frank begins to read it. **Follow up: How does Anne describe her life in hiding?** Possible response: Anne couldn't do normal childhood activities and Father could not work in his business. All Jews had to wear yellow stars on their clothes as identification. Anne's family and the Van Daans had to remain hidden while they were being protected by her father's former employees, Miep and Mr. Kraler.

Page 241
C Vocabulary
Possible answer: *Mercurial* emotions must be emotions that can quickly turn from hot to cold, meaning, one minute Anne might be happy and hyper, while the next minute she might seem unhappy and aloof.

Page 242
A Literary Focus
Possible answer: Mr. Frank tells his wife that they are already doing something illegal by hiding from the Nazis, so she should not be concerned with something as trivial as getting illegal ration books.

Page 243
B Read and Discuss
To introduce the two Jewish families who will share living space, Miep's part as caretaker, and the regulations set up for everyone's safety: **What are we learning in this scene?** Possible response: The two families begin to get settled and Miep and Mr. Kraler bring them some necessities. **Follow up: What part does Miep play in their lives?** Possible response: Miep will come daily with food and she'll check on their needs. The families rely on Miep completely for their well-being. **Follow up: What's life like in the hiding place?** Possible response: While men work on the lower floors of the building, the hideaways must remain quiet and still. From 8am until 6pm, they are trapped and cannot move about.

C Reading Focus

Possible answers: Mr. Kraler and Miep have respect for the Franks, Mr. Frank especially. They are sad to see the Franks forced to go into hiding, but they are ready and willing to help them as best they can. They are brave and compassionate to help out.

D Vocabulary

Here, *interval* means "time between."

Page 244
A Literary Focus

Possible answer: Anne and the others must not make a sound from 8 o'clock in the morning until 6 o'clock at night, or else they risk getting caught. They cannot speak above a whisper, walk around, run water, use the sink or the bathroom, or do anything else that might get them discovered.

Page 245
C Language Coach

Circle: "ly".

D Reading Focus

Possible answer: We can infer that Mr. Frank is trying to stay positive about the situation. He is very serious when he states the rules that they all must follow, but he tries to suggest that their lives in hiding will be just as they were when they lived at home—starting every night at 6 o'clock, when they can talk together and eat together and act like one family.

Page 248
A Literary Focus

Possible answer: Peter can now remove the Star of David from his clothing without being arrested because he is staying in hiding and is not planning on going out anytime soon—so there is no chance that he can get caught.

Page 249
C Language Coach

Underline: "badly"
Circle: "ly"

Page 250
A Reading Focus

Possible answer: We can infer that Peter is a little bit shy and lonely. He tells Anne that he had no friends to meet up with after school. But more importantly, he is a strong character, because he rips the Star of David from his clothing and burns it on the stove, as a way to

protest the Nazi's treatment of Jewish people like himself.

Page 251
C Literary Focus

Possible answer: Anne realizes how serious her situation is when she attempts to go downstairs to the office to fetch a pencil and her father tells her that she cannot ever go beyond their door—not even at night when no one is in the office. Anne cries because she realizes that she must stay trapped and hidden if she is to remain alive.

Page 253
B Language Coach

Underline: "quickly" or "comfortingly."
Circle: "ly"/ *Quickly* means "at a fast or rapid pace" and *Comfortingly* means "in a way that comforts."

D Read and Discuss

To focus on the difficulties and stress that being in hiding is creating: **What have we learned in this scene?** Possible response: Anne is frightened that they will be caught and imprisoned at any moment, yet she remains optimistic.

Page 254
Skills Practice
Use a Concept Map

Possible answers:
Anne Frank: Anne is only 13 years old, and she is just beginning to learn the significance of her situation. She will relate her life in hiding to us through her diary entries.
Otto Frank: Mr. Frank seems to be in charge, relaying rules and information to his family and the Van Daan's to make sure that everyone stays safe.
Miep: Mr. Frank's old business companion who has offered his home to support two Jewish families and protect them from the Nazi party.
Peter Van Daan: The Van Daan child is shy but surprisingly fierce at heart when he burns his Star of David.

Page 255
Applying Your Skills
Literary Focus

1. b   2. c

Reading Focus

Students' answers will vary, but students should draw from their previous answers and inferences to write a paragraph describing one of the play's characters in depth.

Vocabulary Review
1. No   2. Yes   3. Yes

A TRAGEDY REVEALED: A HEROINE'S LAST DAYS

Major Understanding for Read and Discuss Queries: Students should understand that this text is one man's journey to find the truth about Anne Frank's last days. He uses several sources, including interviews with various individuals who knew Anne. (Students may get confused as the author transitions from one source to another). All of these sources support the author's main point, that although Anne suffered more than any human being should ever have to suffer, she never lost her strong spirit and her will to help others.

Page 257
A Read and Discuss
To establish that the narrator found a film that showed Anne Frank before she was forced into hiding, and to draw attention to Anne and her powerful diary: **What have we learned about Anne Frank so far?** Possible response: She had a strong spirit and left behind a diary so powerful it that it has sparked emotion from people as far away as Japan and has been the basis for a famous play as well. She must have been someone really special.

Page 258
B Read and Discuss
To understand that the author followed the trail of Anne Frank trying to find out as much information about her as he could: **What is the author up to, talking to these people?** Possible response: He set out to follow Anne's trail and see why she has become a legend. **Follow up: What did we learn about Anne in this part and how does it connect with what we talked about?** Possible response: We said she was probably special and the narrator now describes her as indomitable, so we know she did have a fierce spirit.

Page 259
C Reading Focus

Possible answer: The author is using a logical order. The author presents details to shape the reader's understanding of Anne and the process he went through to learn more about her. However, the author does not present the details in chronological order, or, the order in which they actually took place.

Page 260
B Read and Discuss
What have we learned about the day of the capture? Possible response: The surviving office workers are giving their accounts of the day the group was captured. They were all working when the Gestapo came in and told them not to move as they searched the office and the other rooms. For some reason, Anne left her diary there. Otto Frank suspects that maybe Anne felt all was lost, so she didn't even bother to retrieve her diary.

D Read and Discuss
To discern the events as told by Anne's father: **What have we learned from Anne's father?** Possible response: Otto Frank, the only survivor from the annex, is retelling the events of that day from his perspective.

Page 261
F Language Coach
Possible answer: There are two syllables in the word *barrack*. It seems surprising that the second syllable is pronounced with more of a 'u' sound than an 'a' sound.

G Read and Discuss
To develop an understanding of the living conditions of the concentration camp and the family's attitudes toward living there: **What information has Mrs. de Wiek given us about the Franks?** Possible response: Otto Frank was a quiet man, but when Anne got sick, he visited her every evening and told her stories for hours. Anne was just like him, and they always both talked about God.

H Reading Focus
Possible answer: Logical order–Mrs. de Wiek recalls the events that unfolded when Anne came to the camp, but she also recalls memories of seeing Anne and Peter in Westerbork.

Page 262
A Read and Discuss

To draw attention to the fact that the families were often separated while being moved to these concentration camps, and many never saw each other again: **What else has Mrs. De Wiek told us about the families?** Possible response: While traveling, many families would be separated, as the men and women were sent to separate concentration camps. She herself was separated from her husband on this last trip and never saw him again. *To reinforce how badly the Jewish people were being treated*: **Follow up: How does this connect with what we already talked about?** Possible response: These were dreadful times for the Jewish people. They weren't being treated as humans, but rather, as property.

B Read and Discuss
To understand that life at the women's concentration camp was just as bad as life at the previous camp: **What are things like at the new concentration camp?** Possible response: It's just as bad – many women are doing hard labor, while thousands of others are being sent to their deaths in the gas chambers.

C Read and Discuss
To understand what it means to "still have your face": **What does Mrs. de Wiek mean when she says that Anne "still had her face"?** Possible response: A doctor once said that people would pull through if they "still had their face," meaning that they could make it if as long as they still had enough feeling in them to survive. Once your face became empty, it meant that you had given up all hope and would die. Anne kept her face until the very end. She never became numb, and she would cry every time she saw people being taken to the gas chamber, while most others had already become numb to that sight.

Page 263
D Reading Focus
The author is using chronological order.

Page 264
A Read and Discuss
To summarize what happened to the members of the "annex": **What have we learned about the Secret Annex group?** Possible response: Most of the people who lived in the annex died at Auschwitz. Only Mr. Frank survived. Anne, Margot, and Mrs. Van Daan were sent to Bergen-Belsen.

B Read and Discuss
To develop an understanding of Bergen-Belsen as it is today: **What picture is the author giving us of Bergen-Belsen as it is today?** Possible response: As the author views the grounds, he describes a very sad place with many graves.

Page 265
C Vocabulary
Misery means "suffering" or "immense sadness."

D Reading Focus
Possible answer: The author uses mostly logical order, with some chronological order mixed in, as well.

Page 266
A Read and Discuss
To again reinforce how desperate the people living in these camps were: **Now what has happened?** Possible response: A woman who knew Anne's family is in the compound next to Anne. She tried to throw some supplies to Anne, but someone else took them before Anne could get to them. **Follow up: How does this story fit in with what we know about these concentration camps?** Possible response: They were awful places, and the people didn't have enough food or clothing, so they resorted to desperate measures, including stealing, to get what they needed.

B Vocabulary
Pitiful means "meager," "lacking," or "deserving pity."

C Read and Discuss
To understand that Anne and her sister both died just three weeks before Bergen-Belsen was liberated: **How did Anne's story end?** Possible response: Unfortunately, she and her sister both died of typhus just three weeks before their camp was liberated.

Page 267
D Reading Focus
Students' answers will vary. Students should determine which type of structural pattern they found easiest to read, and should back up their opinion with examples from the text.

Page 268
Comprehension Wrap-Up
Possible responses:

Holt Adapted Reader Answer Key

1. Anne seemed to have a positive outlook about life, even in the face of the many horrors she experienced. She seemed to find the good in people and care about fellow human beings. Anne's story will be forever preserved because she kept a diary of her experiences.

2. The behavior of the Nazis toward the Jews shows that when people with deep prejudices are allowed to act on their emotions, they will do horrible things. People who say that they hate another group of people may take out their anger by harming them. This type of behavior could be kept in check if people were more understanding of one another and accepting of different races and faiths.

3. The personal accounts of the people who survived the camps are proof that they existed. Also, the former sites of the camps, like Bergen-Belsen, still have signs that the camps were there. The mass graves also prove that millions of people were killed.

Page 269
Applying Your Skills
Informational Text Focus
Possible answers:

1. Order of importance: Readers were able to learn the author's thoughts on the Nazi occupation of Amsterdam and examine the details he later provided which supported that position.

2. Logical order: Sometimes the author broke from using chronological order to supply background information about Anne or the Frank family. Instead, he would present the facts in an order that would smooth out the story and keep similar parts of the story together.

Vocabulary Review
1. b   2. c

SKILLS REVIEW

Page 270
Vocabulary
1. unabashed   2. evident   3. pitiful
4. conspicuous 5. express   6. barrack
7. interval   8. insight   9. legend
10. inexplicable

Page 271
Language Coach
Students should make pronunciation flashcards and practice reading from them aloud with a partner.

Writing Activity
Students' paragraphs will vary, but should state whether they agree or disagree with the author's description of Anne Frank as having a "strong spirit." Students should be sure to include details from the article that support their opinions.

Holt Adapted Reader Answer Key

Pronunciation Guide

Syllabic Symbol	Example Spelled Normally	Syllabic Spelling
a	cat	(kat)
ay	pail	(payl)
ah	lot	(laht)
eh	hen	(hehn)
ee	me	(mee)
ih	willful	(WIHL fuhl)
y	buy	(by)
oh	grow	(groh)
aw	ball	(bawl)
u	book	(buk)
oo	new	(noo)
oy	cloister	(KLOY stur)
ow	house	(hows)
uh	what	(wuht)
u	sure	(shur)
uh	ago, major, lawful	(uh GOH) (MAY juhr) (LAH fuhl)
ch	chalk	(chahk)
sh	show	(shoh)
th	thin, there	(thihn) (thehr)
zh	treasure	(TREH zhur)
ng	sing	(sihng)
l	metal	(MEH tl)
n	sudden	(SUH dn)
f	phone	(fohn)
k	can	(kan)
s	certain	(SUR tuhn)
g	get	(geht)
j	germ	(jurm)

Literary, Reading, and Informational Text Skills

The lists on the following pages show the literary, reading, and informational text skills taught in *The Holt Reader, Adapted Version* Introductory Through Second Course.

Introductory Course

Literary Skills

Characterization and External Conflicts 76
Dialogue and Stage Directions 226
Evaluating a Story's Credibility 100
Figurative Language 216
First-Person and Third-Person
  Point of View 116
Forms of Fiction: Novella 10

Forms of Fiction: The Short Story 2
Literary Devices 122, 132, 138
Plot and Setting 54
Repetition and Refrain 210
Rhyme and Rhyme Scheme 202
Theme 94

Reading Skills

Author's Purpose 116
Compare Authors' Purposes 122, 132, 138
Evaluating a Writer's Conclusions 170
Finding the Theme 94
Making and Adjusting Predictions 10
Making and Supporting Assertions 176
Making Generalizations 100

Making Predictions 2
Questioning 210
Reading a Poem 202
Re-reading 216
Sequencing 54
Visualizing 76, 226

Informational Text Focus

Analyzing Fallacious Reasoning 186
Analyzing Persuasive Techniques 182
Analyzing Propaganda 192
Comparison and Contrast 84
Connecting Main Ideas
  Across Texts 154, 162
Outlining and Summarizing 67

Persuasion 170
Preparing an Application 108
Recognizing Types of Evidence 176
Structural Features of a Magazine 32
Structural Features of a Newspaper 38
Structural Features of a Web Site 44
Taking Notes 64

First Course

Second Course

Literary Skills

Reading Skills

Informational Text Focus

High Frequency

Word Lists

First Hundred Words

the	he	go	who
a	I	see	an
is	they	then	their
you	one	us	she
to	good	no	new
and	me	him	said
we	about	by	did
that	had	was	boy
in	if	come	three
not	some	get	down
for	up	or	work
at	her	two	put
with	do	man	were
it	when	little	before
on	so	has	just
can	my	them	long
will	very	how	here
are	all	like	other
of	would	our	old
this	any	what	take
your	been	know	cat
as	out	make	again
but	there	which	give
be	from	much	after
have	day	his	many

Second Hundred Words

saw	big	may	fan
home	where	let	five
soon	am	use	read
stand	ball	these	over
box	morning	right	such
upon	live	present	way
first	four	tell	too
came	last	next	shall
girl	color	please	own
house	away	leave	most
find	red	hand	sure
because	friend	more	thing
made	pretty	why	only
could	eat	better	near
book	want	under	than
look	year	while	open
mother	white	should	kind
run	got	never	must
school	play	each	high
people	found	best	far
night	left	another	both
into	men	seem	end
say	bring	tree	also
think	wish	name	until
back	black	dear	call

Third Hundred Words

ask	hat	off	fire
small	car	sister	ten
yellow	write	happy	order
show	try	once	part
goes	myself	didn't	early
clean	longer	set	fat
buy	those	round	third
thank	hold	dress	same
sleep	full	tell	love
letter	carry	wash	hear
jump	eight	start	eyes
help	sing	always	door
fly	warm	anything	clothes
don't	sit	around	through
fast	dog	close	o'clock
cold	ride	walk	second
today	hot	money	water
does	grow	turn	town
face	cut	might	took
green	seven	hard	pair
every	woman	along	now
brown	funny	bed	keep
coat	yes	fine	head
six	ate	sat	food
gave	stop	hope	yesterday

Fourth Hundred Words

told	yet	word	airplane
Miss	true	almost	without
father	above	thought	wear
children	still	send	Mr.
land	meet	receive	side
interest	since	pay	poor
feet	number	nothing	lost
garden	state	need	wind
done	matter	mean	Mrs.
country	line	late	learn
different	large	half	held
bad	few	fight	front
across	hit	enough	built
yard	cover	feet	family
winter	window	during	began
table	even	gone	air
story	city	hundred	young
I'm	together	week	ago
tried	sun	between	world
horse	life	change	kill
brought	street	being	ready
shoes	party	care	stay
government	suit	answer	won't
sometimes	remember	course	paper
time	something	against	outside

Fifth Hundred Words

hour	grade	egg	spell
glad	brother	ground	beautiful
follow	remain	afternoon	sick
company	milk	feed	became
believe	several	boat	cry
begin	war	plan	finish
mind	able	question	catch
pass	charge	fish	floor
reach	either	return	stick
month	less	sir	great
point	train	fell	guess
rest	cost	fill	bridge
sent	evening	wood	church
talk	note	add	lady
went	past	ice	tomorrow
bank	room	chair	snow
ship	flew	watch	whom
business	office	alone	women
whole	cow	low	among
short	visit	arm	road
certain	wait	dinner	farm
fair	teacher	hair	cousin
reason	spring	service	bread
summer	picture	class	wrong
fill	bird	quite	age

Sixth Hundred Words

become	themselves	thousand	wife
body	herself	demand	condition
chance	idea	however	aunt
act	drop	figure	system
die	river	case	line
real	smile	increase	cause
speak	son	enjoy	marry
already	bat	rather	possible
doctor	fact	sound	supply
step	sort	eleven	pen
itself	king	music	perhaps
nine	dark	human	produce
baby	whose	court	twelve
minute	study	force	rode
ring	fear	plant	uncle
wrote	move	suppose	labor
happen	stood	law	public
appear	himself	husband	consider
heart	strong	moment	thus
swim	knew	person	least
felt	often	result	power
fourth	toward	continue	mark
I'll	wonder	price	voice
kept	twenty	serve	whether
well	important	national	president

Notes